Apple Pies and Other Lies

A critical look at sexuality in teen movies from the Nineties and Noughties.

By Vanessa Bowen

Apple Pies and Other Lies

For information contact :

Vanessa Bowen

http://www.nessbow.com

Book and Cover design by Cassie Daley

ISBN: 978-0-6457259-0-2

First Edition: July 2023

10 9 8 7 6 5 4 3 2 1

CONTENTS

Introduction

The 90's were a fantastic time to be a movie-loving teenager. The cinemas were bombarded with a tidal wave of awesome teen films. From coming-of-age stories to puppy-love romances, from bawdy comedies and high-school dramas, the box office was flooded with teen movies on a grand scale. Although Teen Movies have been around since the 1950's, the 1980's saw an explosion of movies aimed at teenagers. These Teen Movies starred adolescent characters and told stories that felt relevant to teen audiences. With the success of movies like Pretty in Pink, The Breakfast Club and Sixteen Candles, Teen Movies morphed into their own genre of film. By the 90's and early 2000's a new breed of Teen Movies had emerged. - a breed that was raunchier and bolder than their 1980's counterparts. For those of us who grew up in the 1990's and 2000's there was a huge array of teen movies to enjoy. While some of us flocked to the cinema during summer holidays, the ready availability of VHS rentals offered the opportunity to watch at slumber parties with your mates or while stretched out on the sofa on a lazy weekend afternoon.

I was a 90's kid myself. A movie-lover from the moment of my first viewing of The Wizard of Oz, I eagerly lapped up the offerings from my local Video Ezy, recorded Friday night movies back-to-back on VCR tapes bought with my pocket money and lived for summer holiday trips to the cinema. I lost count of the number of times I watched Clueless and was able to quote Can't Hardly Wait line-for-line. I vividly recall my first viewing of American Pie, a film my parents had absolutely forbidden me to watch but which a friend had managed to convince her mother to hire for us. My weekends and school holidays were punctuated with movie after movie, and lunchtimes at school were spent discussing my favourites with my friends.

In those days I did more than just watch films, I absorbed them. The costumes, the music and the slang all seeped into my brain and influenced how I dressed, what I listened to and how I spoke. Conversely, the lessons of these films had a profound effect on my own ideas and beliefs. In particular, I can look back on this time and see how strongly my constant diet of teen films influenced by thoughts about relationships and sex.

The teen films of the 90's and noughties were bolder and brassier than their 80's counterparts. They were much more overt in their discussion of the topic of sex. The characters in these films were more self-assured, more confident and more blatantly sexual than most teenage characters to grace the screen previously. As the decade wore on, movies in the teen genre began to feature more graphic depictions of sexuality. Curious young minds such as my own often looked to these films to answer their questions about sex, and so many of our ideas about what is "normal" in sex and relationships were based on scenes from these teen flicks.

Our teen years are a fascinating time of rapid development. Not only is it the time when most people begin to start making sense of their own sexuality[1] but for many of us it's the first time we begin to exercise agency over our identity. It's a point in our lives when we are figuring out who we are and trying on different versions of the person we will become. Adolescence is a time of curiosity, of seeking

---

[1] Greydanus & Omar (2014). 10.

answers to the innumerable questions that are bubbling inside our skulls. As teens we are hungry to know more about the world beyond our own backyards. The media we consume during this time has a huge influence on our ideas, values and beliefs. There can be little doubt that the media we consume influences our ideas on sexual norms as well.

What we know about sex is rarely the result of a single source. Most of us tend to ferret out information from a variety of places: the copies of Cosmopolitan stacked on our aunt's coffee table, the stories our friends tell us, the snippets of adult conversations overheard. These pieces are melded together with more formal education, such as school sex-ed classes, the Birds-and- Bees talks with parents and so forth. We gather up and mesh all this information into a kind of Sexual Gestalt, the ultimate product of our sum total knowledge about sex. For those of us who grew up on a steady diet of teen flicks, these too contributed to our Sexual Gestalt and therefore have influenced what we think we know about sex.

In the late 90's and early 2000's, sexual education in schools was still largely focused on abstinence-only programs. These programs emphasized teaching children the harmful psychological and physical effects of premarital sex and positing abstinence as the best course of action. [2] Naturally, these education programs often gloss over or omitted altogether certain subjects, such as contraception, masturbation and pleasure. A study conducted during this time found that half of USA high school students stated that they were lacking information about Sexually Transmitted Infections, and 40% said they didn't have enough information about birth control.[3] And when teens have questions, they go looking for answers.

If answers regarding sexuality can't be found at school, there are a number of other sources a teenager might turn to. If they feel comfortable enough to do so, they may ask their parents. However, many parents feel uncomfortable talking to their teenagers about sex or may echo the abstinence-only lessons that they've learned at school. Teens may turn to their

---

[2] Kuo (2000). 138.
[3] Kim, L.L. (1999).

peer group, seeking the advice of older, more experienced friends or pooling what information they've each been able to glean from whatever sources are available. Some teenagers seek to satisfy their curiosity by looking at pornography.[4] More commonly though, mainstream media such as television programs and movies are used to answer the questions a teenager might have about sex.[5] In a 2003 study, 39% of teenagers said that the television and movies were a primary source of sexual information for them.[6] When young people don't have comprehensive sex education, they seek to fill the gaps in their knowledge using movies and television.

This is problematic because these types of media aren't intended to educate, they're meant to entertain. Movies aren't an accurate source of information about sex and sexuality, and it's easy for a teenager who is trying to educate themselves through this medium to end up with the wrong end of the stick. There's a huge difference between reality and what looks good

---

[4] Greydanus & Omar (2014). 33.
[5] Kunkel Et Al (1999)
[6] McElderry & Omar. 2003.

on screen. Depictions of sex in television and film are more likely to show sexually irresponsible behaviour because that generates a more interesting or engaging narrative.[7] The truth might be a lot less hilarious or dramatic than the scene the director wants to create. With that being said, there are grains of truth buried within these depictions of sex. Media depictions of sex also inform our beliefs about what sex should be like, and the deeper values about sex and sexuality. And the more we are exposed to these messages, the more our internal values and beliefs are shaped by them.[8] The stories we tell through media influence what we, as a culture, believe to be "normal".[9]

As a person who is fascinated by films and sexuality, I felt inspired to take a trip back down memory lane and examine the teen films of the 90's and 2000's in relation to their depictions of sexuality. I wanted to look more closely at how they shaped my own beliefs about sex and compare and contrast the content to the actual experience of teenagers who watched these

---

[7] Mohamad. (2014).
[8] Mohamad (2014)
[9] Corliss. (2017)

films. I have chosen to look at a variety of movies from 1995 – 2006 that feature characters aged 13-23 and examine how they portray sexuality, and the accuracy of that portrayal. With the power of hindsight, I want to take a look back at the teen films of the 1990s and 2000s to examine these films to find out what's real, what's not and how these iconic films from my teen years influenced my ideas about sexuality.

11

Chapter 1

Parental Approaches to Teen Sexuality

"I'm not a regular mom, I'm a cool mom" - Mean Girls.

Adolescence often tests the bonds between teens and their parents. It's reportedly the most stressful of all the developmental ages for parents.[10] It's a time of rapid change, of pulling away from childhood and stepping towards adulthood. While teenagers might be eager to establish themselves as independent adults, their parents are often reluctant to let go. It can be difficult to accept that the child they love is growing and maturing, and the amount of care and protection they need is waning with each passing year. The dichotomous nature of the relationship: a teenager longing to tread their own path and a parent

---

[10] Pasley & Gecas (1984).

eager to protect and guide them; can create a fraught environment at home.

When it comes to sexuality, parents are faced with a myriad of difficult choices with regards to their teenagers. Parents must choose how to talk to their children about sex, what information they will give them at what age and what values they want to impart to their children around sex. It can be extremely challenging for parents to accept that their children are developing sexually, and evidence of their offspring's burgeoning sexuality can be confronting. Teen movies display a wide range of parental attitudes and approaches to managing conversations around sex and protecting their children from real or perceived dangers around sexuality. Many parents are unsure how to feel about teenage sex and are torn between wanting to discourage the behaviour and wishing to provide information and guidance. [11]

Parental attitudes to teen sexuality seem to fall into two broad categories. Firstly, you have the parent who

---

[11] Kuo, (2000), 191.

doesn't believe that their teenager should be having sex at all and takes measures to prevent their teen from engaging in sexual behaviour. On the other end of the spectrum, you have parents who want to encourage sexual expression, who facilitate an open-door policy when it comes to discussing sex.

In the teen films from the nineties and noughties, we see examples of both of these attitudes. Most often though, we see an approach that falls somewhere between these two extremes. There are plenty of examples of parents who are willing to accept that their teenager is having sex but does not want to know any details or who turns a blind eye to their child's developing sexuality. While they don't necessarily disapprove of the behaviour, they don't actively encourage it either.

The sex negative parent

Some parents take a firm stance that teenagers should not be having sex. This opinion may be based on moral reasons, religious reasons or practical reasons. Such parents may refuse to discuss sexuality at all with their children, or choose to only focus on the potential negative consequences of sex. Parents may choose to set rigid rules in an attempt to prevent their child from engaging in sexualized behaviour.

Often, such measures will be put in place as a way to protect the teenager from unwanted consequences of sex, such as unplanned pregnancy or sexually transmitted diseases. Parents who choose to attempt to limit information about sex and control their children's interactions may do so with the best intentions. However, there is little evidence to suggest that parental disapproval will actually stop teenagers from having sex. It does seem clear that if parents have shown a negative or prohibitive attitude towards sex, their children are less likely to talk to them about sex or seek their assistance if they find themselves in trouble.[12] Additionally, children of parents who fail to communicate effectively about sex are more likely to engage in risky sexual behaviour.[13] There is no indication that teens who are raised in this environment are less likely to have sex, only that they

---

[12] Kuo, (2000), 195.
[13] Afifi, Joseph & Aldeis. (2008).

are unlikely to ask their parents for information or seek their assistance if they wind up in a difficult situation.

In the crop of movies which I examined, there are plenty of examples of parents who take a sex negative approach, prohibiting their children from having sex and trying to frighten them away from expressing their sexuality. This type of parenting is often shown when there are additional cultural or religious considerations at play. Such examples include A Walk to Remember (2002) and Bend it Like Beckham (2002). In A Walk to Remember, the protagonist's father is a Reverend and sees it as his moral duty to ensure that his daughter understands the importance of maintaining her virginity. In Bend it Like Beckham, the main character, Jasminder, is dealing with pressures from her Indian family who bemoan the dangers of her playing football with boys and walking around with her legs bare. In both cases, cultural and religious values play into the parent's desire to protect their child and educate them about the perceived dangers of sex. Cultural and religious factors are an important determining factor about the way a parent will talk to their children about sex and the type of information they will impart.[14]

Interestingly, the sex negative parent trope seems to occur most frequently in films where the teen protagonist is female. There are numerous examples of film parents trying to control their daughter's sexuality, to impose strict rules and frighten them into chastity. I can surmise a few possible reasons for this. Firstly, female virginity seems to be more valuable and more closely guarded than male virginity (I will discuss this in more detail later in this book). Secondly, girls are more likely to be negatively impacted by the unwanted consequences of teenage sex than boys. For example, unplanned pregnancy has a more significant physical, emotional and social impact on girls than boys. Research into parental communication about sex has shown that while parents of girls are more likely to communicate about sex, they are also more prone to highlighting the negative aspects of sex such as unwanted pregnancy and STIs.[15]

---

[14] Cui (2016).
[15] Otto (2020).

In The Virgin Suicides (2000) the Lisbon family consists of two very strict parents and five teenage daughters. The film chronicles the neighborhood's fascination with the Lisbon girls, and their parents increasingly extreme measures to try to protect their daughters from the perceived evils of the world. The Lisbons are shown to be a religious family, they attend church and their pastor visits the house on a number of occasions. Mr and Mrs Lisbon put strict rules in place in an attempt to limit their daughter's social connections and activities. The girls are required to be chaperoned when they attend dances and parties, they are to dress modestly and any prospective dates must ask parental permission before taking the girls out. The narrator recalls a time when Mrs Lisbon became furious upon discovering that Lux, their fourteen-year-old daughter, has written her crush's name in permanent marker on all of her underpants. In an attempt to expunge this boy from Lux's consciousness, Mrs Lisbon orders her to bleach the initials out of all the panties. Ironically, the Lisbon's rules do not seem to prevent their daughter's from engaging in sexual exploration, but only serves to make them more secretive about it.

One of the most well-known examples of a parent exercising strict rules to protect their teenage daughters from unplanned pregnancy is Mr Stratford from 10 Things I Hate About You (1999). Mr Stratford works as a gynecologist and spends most of his days "up to his elbows in placenta". His profession seems to have instilled in him a strong desire to protect his daughters from teenage pregnancy and the perceived pitfalls of the same. To this end, he imposes a strict rule that they are not allowed to date until they graduate. Mr Stratford is also seen using fear tactics to try to dissuade his daughters from having sex, such as telling them horror stories from his workday. While Mr Stratford's methods are somewhat extreme, it's clear that his actions come from a place of genuine love and concern for his daughters. He's trying to protect them from the world and is having difficulty relaxing his grip and allowing them to make their own decisions.

Sex negative parenting may show up as a parent refusing to discuss sex with their child, or giving their teenager misinformation when they ask about sex. In Now and Then (1995) Chrissy's mother is horrified when Chrissy asks her what sex is. She responds by telling her that she's too young to know and it's scary that she asked. Chrissy's mother then explains sex using a gardening metaphor, which only leaves Chrissy more confused. In Riding in Cars With Boys (2002), Mrs Donofrio tells her daughter that if a boy puts his tongue in her mouth, it's because he wants her to bite it off. The Donofrio's show a distinct disappointment and disgust when their fifteen-year-old daughter, Beverly, is caught having sex in the backseat of a car. Their disgust overflows to anger when Beverly becomes pregnant, and they keep her at arms-length for decades afterwards. This example is consistent with the finding that parental disapproval towards sex isn't likely to discourage teenagers to have sex, but it does reduce the likelihood that they'll come to their parents for help regarding sexual matters.[16]

---

[16] Kuo (2000), 195.

Although the desire to encourage teenagers to wait until they're older to start having sex may stem from the belief that early sexual behaviour is risky, this may not necessarily be the case. If a teenager has been given accurate sexual education and is raised in an environment that encourages them to take responsibility for themselves in sexual situations, this may mitigate the potential risks. Rather, a teenager who has been given a comprehensive sex education may feel empowered to explore their sexuality earlier, but they may be more likely to be responsible and safe during this exploration. Sexual behaviour is risky when the teenagers involved have not been armed with accurate information about sex and the confidence to advocate for themselves when having sex.[17] Therefore, it would seem that parents who are seeking to protect their children from the negative consequences of sex would be more successful if they take the time to teach their children about contraceptives, effective communication and responsible sexuality, rather than trying to frighten them or deter them from having sex in the first place.

---

[17] Cui (2016).

The sex positive parent

On the other hand, there are a number of parents who choose to take a more open stance on sexuality. Some households attempt to create a sex positive atmosphere to encourage teenagers to ask questions and offer honest and frank answers. It seems that many parents who were raised with an attitude of shame and fear around sex often strive to do better with their own children, attempting to create a sex positive environment at home.[18] Parents who take such an approach might allow a teenager to have a partner spend the night or assist with the purchase of contraceptives. This type of parenting can be very effective in promoting positive sexual behaviour. Debra Haffner, president of the Sexuality Information and Education Council of the United States stated that parents who communicate openly about sex and set clear limits raise teenagers who are more likely to abstain and who are more likely to practice safer sex if they do choose to have sex.[19] Rather than encouraging teens to have sex, providing them with

---

[18] Hockersmith (2016).
[19] Wingert, (1999). 80,81.

information and a sex-positive environment seems to empower them to make better choices.

Possibly one of the best examples of sex positive parenting in film is Jim's father from the American Pie franchise. Jim's father is open and loving, encouraging his son to ask questions about sex and attempting to create a dialogue about sexuality without shame and embarrassment. When he walks in on Jim masturbating, he is initially shocked but quickly reassures Jim that masturbation is natural and normal. He doesn't shame his son for experimenting and maintains Jim's privacy by not telling his mother. Jim's father attempts to encourage his son's sexuality by buying him pornographic magazines and giving an impromptu female anatomy lesson using them as visual aids (much to Jim's horror). When he finds condoms in Jim's drawer, he is initially taken aback, but then expresses his relief that Jim is taking precautions. In the sequel, he reassures and supports Jim during a visit to the emergency room following a sexual mishap and stands up for him when other patients express disgust at Jim's sexuality. Although Jim's father is notoriously awkward in his approach, he fosters a loving and open relationship with his son which encourages Jim to turn to his father in times of need. Jim feels like he can ask his dad for advice and knows that he has someone to seek support from when things (inevitably) go wrong.

Looking for Alibrandi (1999) shows a more down-to-earth version of the sex positive parent. Josie Alibrandi is close to her mother Christina, and they have regular and frank discussions about sex. Christina is shown to be somewhat protective of her daughter, most likely because Josie is the result of her own teen pregnancy. This is noteworthy, as parents may struggle to share their own experiences with their children if they feel like they made mistakes in their own youth.[20] Although Christina has a desire to shield Josie from the pain she endured as a teenage parent, she trusts her to make her own decision and respects her enough to answer her questions. Although their discussions aren't as explicit as those in American Pie, and there is an undercurrent of morality (as they are

---

[20] Hockersmith (2016).

Catholic) the Alibrandi household is conservatively sex positive.

The thing that differentiates a sex positive parent from a sex ambivalent one is that the sex positive parent has a genuine wish to be a part of their child's sexual journey. They want to be the person that their teenager comes to with questions and actively seeks to foster this relationship. Unlike the "don't ask, don't tell" attitude of the sex ambivalent parent, the sex positive parent maintains an open-door policy on all questions relating to sex. In Ginger Snaps (2000) the mother is thrilled when her daughters come to her for advice about sex. She is genuinely touched that her children felt comfortable enough to come to her with their questions and fears. Get Over it (2001) features a set of parents who work as sexuality educators who have worked hard to create a sex positive relationship with their son. This film shows parents with unique expertise in the area of sexuality, who have confidence and experience discussing sexual topics. This sets them apart from most film and real-life parents, who might find their own knowledge and confidence to be a barrier to discussing sexuality with their teenage children.

Studies have shown that parents talking to their children about sex is most effective when it's done frequently and in an informal setting.21 Rather than having a single, stilted conversation about sex, parents should aim to create an open dialogue about sexuality, discussing it often and without embarrassment or shame. Taking a more casual approach to discussing sex removes a lot of the stigma and shame around the topic of sex and produces teens who feel more comfortable asking questions and seeking more information when required. In several of the films I've discussed, we see sex positive parents who try to create this more informal dialogue. The best example is found in Looking for Alibrandi, where Josie feels comfortable asking her mother questions and they have relaxed conversations about sex while Christina styles Josie's hair or cooks dinner. In American Pie, Jim's father attempts to make their talks casual and laid back, but Jim still feels embarrassed

---

21 Otto (2020).

talking to his Dad about sex. His father still makes a valiant effort to give Jim a comprehensive sex education and provide him with an outlet for questions and advice.

The sex ambivalent parent

The sex ambivalent parent's approach to managing their child's sexuality tends to be in between the two previously discussed methods. While they don't actively disapprove of their teenager having sex, they also don't appear to encourage it. The sex ambivalent parent may be embarrassed or uncomfortable talking about sex with their children, or may have difficulty seeing their teenagers as sexual beings. Parents might feel ill-equipped to answer their questions about sex and may therefore point them to alternative sources of information.

We often see examples in film of parents who accept that their children have likely had sex, but really don't want to know any details about their kid's sex lives. In Mallrats (1995) Mr Svenning confronts his daughter's boyfriend, T.S, growling "You two have been seeing one another long enough for you to have slimed your way into her panties". Mr Svenning seems vaguely disgusted at the idea that his daughter would have deigned to have had sex with T.S, but he's willing to accept that the act has probably happened.

Some parents who fall within the "sex ambivalent" category will take similar measures as their sex positive counterparts. For example, they may purchase condoms and keep them in the bathroom where they are easily accessible. As opposed to the sex positive parent, who aims to encourage sexual expression and empowered decisions, the sex neutral parent may be more likely to take such measures as a harm reduction technique. It could be that they don't' feel as though they're able to stop their children from having sex, but they feel that they can protect them from harm if they provide a safe environment and contraceptives.[22] In the movie Crazy/Beautiful (2001), the main character's parents have a stash of condoms in the medicine cabinet. Nicole, the protagonist, boldly collects a condom from the supply and takes it

---

[22] Kuo. (2000) 174.

to her room before a sexual encounter with her new partner. Interestingly, Nicole states afterwards that her father "doesn't care" if she has sex, suggesting that while the condoms have been made available, it's not a sign that her parents are encouraging her to have sex. Rather, it seems that they want her to be safe if she does decide to make that choice.

Alternatively, sex ambivalent parents may feel uncomfortable discussing sex or may lack confidence in their ability to communicate with their teenager.[23] We see this play out in numerous films where the parental figure's discussions around sex are stilted and use a lot of evasive language around the subject. For example, in Son in Law, Rebecca's father tries to talk to her about sex before she goes to college, but only manages to say that "The lifestyle is much faster" in college, seemingly unable to elaborate. These examples show parents who want to be able to talk with their children about sex, but seem unsure of how to approach the subject, and feel a lot of embarrassment and shame when it comes to

---

[23] Otto (2020).

discussing sex. It may also be challenging for parents to talk to their children about sex if they feel that their own knowledge on the topic is lacking. If a parent feels like they aren't able to confidently provide information or answer questions about sexuality, they may avoid the topic altogether. Hockersmith (2016) highlights the importance of parents being willing to do their own research, to seek out the gaps in their own knowledge in order to better educate their children.

My personal experience is closest to the "sex ambivalent parent" scenario that I've discussed. While both of my parents wanted to protect me and provide me with information about sexuality, I know that they felt uncomfortable discussing such topics with me. My mother was raised in a Catholic household. She told me that her own sex education was taught by nuns and the basic message was "This is what sex is, now don't you dare do it!" She has also told me that she wanted to provide her children with better sex education than she had access to when she was a teenager, but lacked confidence in discussing sexual topics with her kids. My sex education at home usually comprised my parents presenting me with a book written for children that covered topics such as sex or puberty. I was left to my own devices to read the book, and then my parents were open to me asking any questions that arose during my reading. While I do remember asking my parents questions about sex, it was always a pretty uncomfortable experience for everyone involved. I was much more likely to try to find the answer myself by checking in library books or reading the sealed sections of Dolly and Girlfriend magazine. My parents never took issue with me having these books in the house and seemed happy with me taking my sex education into my own hands. I was much more likely to turn to my friends when I had questions, rather than asking Mum and Dad.

While I acknowledge that my parents did the best they could with the tools at their disposal, there are times when I wish I had been raised in a more sex positive household. Doing my own research into sex education left a lot of room for misunderstanding and misinformation. As an adult, I've often found gaps in my sexual knowledge, or learned that things I thought I knew about sex were actually dead wrong. Usually, this misunderstanding came from me piecing together bits of vague information to create an incomplete whole. If I'd had access to more comprehensive sex education, I might have relied less on teen films and magazines to teach me about sex, and I think it's likely that my overall attitude towards sex might have been a bit more rounded as I moved into adulthood.

It seems to me that the teen films of the 90's and 2000's did a decent job of depicting the differing parental approaches to teaching teens about sex. It is my hope that as the kids who grew up during this period begin having kids of their own, that their approach will lean more towards Jim's Dad and further away from Mr Stratford, and that more children of this generation will be raised in sex positive households.

Chapter 2
Talking with Peers About Sex

"This one time, at Band Camp...", American Pie.

During my teenage years, the relationship I had with my friends held a great deal of significance. I shared everything with my friends, from classes at school to extracurricular interests. We would spend our weekends and holidays together, and most nights after school were taken up chatting on the phone or meeting at one another's houses. I can't remember another period in my life when friendships were as close or meaningful. In my twenties I poured a great deal of time and energy into developing romantic partnerships, and during my childhood I spent the bulk of my time with my family. But in those adolescent years, my friends reigned supreme in my world.

Similarly, in teen films from the 1990's and 2000s, the friendship group is often depicted as the most significant relationship in the character's life. It's very common to see stories that explore the dynamics of a friendship group, or to have the protagonist's best friend act as their sidekick and confidante. The friendship group we belong to can indicate status or affiliation with social subcultures. In high school, friends become our chosen family, and we turn to them in good times and bad.

During this point in our lives, we share everything with friends, including sex. Teens commonly talk to their friends about sex and may glean a lot of their sexual education from their friends. While researching this book, I noticed three trends regarding the way that teenagers talk to their friends about sex.

Pooling your knowledge

As I've discussed previously, teenagers tend to gather their sexual education from a variety of sources. When they haven't received comprehensive sex education at school and if their parents haven't provided opportunities for education and exploration, then teenagers tend to seek answers elsewhere. It is not at all uncommon for teenagers to discuss sexuality with their friends, looking for answers as a group and trying to piece together the full picture from the limited information that they have each managed to gather. This is problematic because often their peers are less likely to have accurate information and are a less reliable source of sexual education.[24] One of the best film examples of this type of information sharing is depicted in Now and Then. In this film, a friendship group of four pre-teen girls spend practically every day of their summer holidays together. A lot of the film is devoted to exploring the relationships within their friendship group, as the four of them start showing an interest in boys and sexuality. Of the four, the character Teeny (portrayed by Thora Birch) is the most sexually precocious. She is confident and forthright and acts as the ringleader of the group. Teeny prides herself on her vast knowledge about sex and relationships, which has mostly been gathered from pilfered copies of Cosmopolitan and snippets she's

---

[24] Cui (2016).

overheard from adult conversations. On numerous occasions, Teeny attempts to educate her friends about sex and answer their questions.

There is one particularly funny scene where the girls stumble upon some boys swimming naked, and huddle behind a bush to talk about their penises. Teeny tells her friends that when a man's penis gets hard, it grows to a foot long. Chrissy, the meekest of the four, the mortified and Teeny admonishes her because her mother never taught her anything about sex. Teeny sees herself as the educator of the group, even though the information that she's disseminating is dead wrong. These scenes illustrate findings which show that young people often rely on sources outside formal education to fill in the gaps of their sexual knowledge, even if the information they receive from these sources is not valid.[25]

In American Pie, Kevin asks his older brother's advice on how to make his girlfriend orgasm. His brother gifts him a homemade sex manual, a collaborative

---

[25] Norwick (2016).

effort by his friends and classmates. The manual contains detailed information about sexual techniques and answers a lot of Kevin's questions about relationships and intercourse. The manual is a physical manifestation of the sharing of information about sex. It is quite literally a book made of the pasted-together tidbits that each author has managed to gather and is passed from person to person to educate. This trope mirrors the real-life scenario of young people sharing the information they've gathered about sex and attempting to help one another figure it out when there isn't a reliable adult source to learn from.

The sexual mentor

An extension of the idea of learning about sex from your friends is the trope of the "Sexual Mentor". In many of the films I watched while researching this book, there is one friend who is more mature and experienced than the others. Their sexual experience and knowledge give them a kind of social capital, a special status that elevates them above their less sexually precocious friends. This person (or persons, as there may be more than one) acts as a mentor to the less experienced friends, answering their questions and providing guidance as they begin to venture into their own sexual explorations. This trope is shown in both male and female friendship groups and is not predominantly skewed towards one gender in particular.

In American Pie, there is a definite sexual hierarchy in the group of four male protagonists. While they are all virgins, some are more sexually experienced than others. Jim and Finch are the least experienced, and Jim in particular seems to look up to his friends for guidance and advice. Both Oz and Kevin have had sexual interactions with women and have experienced oral sex and digital penetration. One particularly memorable example of the less-experienced friends seeking guidance from their mentors occurs in the scene where Jim asks them both what third base feels like and Oz tells him that it's like "warm apple pie". The group are very tight-knit and encourage one another in their quest to have sex. They seem to see sharing this information as a way to give their buddies a leg-up.

American Pie also depicts a similar dynamic between female friends. We see Jessica supporting Vicky as she begins to contemplate having sex for the first time. Jessica has had sex with several people and acts as a kind of sexual mentor, passing advice to Vicky, answering her questions about whether sex is going to hurt and encouraging her to go for it when she feels ready.

A number of other films show more experienced women helping their friends prepare to lose their virginity. In Mona Lisa Smile, Giselle is the most sexually precocious of the group and acts as a role model for Connie. Connie is a virgin but feels swept up by the idea of romance. Connie deeply desires the kind of erotic adventures that Giselle is known for. Giselle shares her knowledge about contraceptives and encourages Giselle to flirt with the boy that she has a crush on. In Empire Records, virginal Corey asks her best friend, Gina, for advice about having sex for the first time. Gina helps Corey plan for her first time, even loaning her a sexy red bra to wear for the occasion. These representations recognise the importance of the sexual debut, and show more experienced friends as playing an encouraging role in assisting their friends to prepare for their first time.

Even outside the context of virginity, we see many examples of the more experienced friend acting as a kind of mentor and educator for their friends. In Looking for Alibrandi, the main friendship group is made up of three girls: Sarah, who is sexually confident; Josie, who is interested in sex but isn't yet ready to lose her virginity; and Ana who is committed to remaining a virgin until she is married. The three girls come from similarly religious backgrounds where there is a lack of sexual education and few opportunities to ask questions about the mechanics of sex. Sarah acts as a kind of de facto sex educator for the group, passing on the knowledge she's gathered from her vast sexual experience. Josie and Ana's sex education is largely gleaned from a combination of what they've read in magazines and what Sarah has shared about her own exploits.

In Clueless, Tai is the only member of the group who has had sex. As Dionne becomes more adventurous in her own relationship, she begins asking Tai for her advice. It is common to see groups of close-knit friends in films where the more mature and experienced friends take care of the less precocious friends, offering advice and encouragement and supplementing their sex education with their own advice and tips. This type of relationship may be a healthy way for teenagers to share experiences and feel supported as they move towards being ready to explore sexually.

Kiss and tell

Another way that sex may be discussed with friends in films is through comparing experiences and bragging. This is particularly common in films that feature groups of male protagonists, as sexual experience and prowess may be seen as a measure of status. Bragging about your conquests is a way of proving your worth and showing your mates how virile and manly you are. In American Pie, this type of interaction is hinted at when a young girl says that she's hesitant to have sex with Stifler because she doesn't want to be "some girl you go bragging to all your friends about". Later in the film, Heather becomes angry at Oz when she mistakenly thinks that he's been laughing with his friends about her. The female characters in this film seem well aware of the likelihood that their male partners will tell their friends about their sexual exploits.

It would seem that this type of male bragging isn't limited to the 1990's and early 2000's. In fact, there is plenty of evidence to suggest that young men have been sharing their sexual success stories with their mates for centuries. In 1996's Romeo and Juliet, we first meet Romeo when he is talking to his friends about the woman he is infatuated with, and the group debates her beauty and the likelihood that Romeo would be successful if he propositions her. Although the film was made and is set in the 90's, it is based on a text that is 400 years older, showing that even centuries apart, this type of bawdy banter hasn't changed.

In Road Trip, the protagonist, Josh, is encouraged by his male friends to try to sleep with Beth, a gorgeous woman who is clearly smitten with him. When Josh succeeds in bedding Beth, he rushes to tell his friends and is even willing to let them watch a video tape of them having sex. It would seem that for young men, the act of sharing their sexual adventures with their friends is an integral part of the experience. If the sex was bad, then the group will commiserate and try to think of ways to make it better next time. But if it was good, then they've earned bragging rights over their friends. This kind of sexual one-upmanship is very common in the teen movies of the 1990's and early 2000's, and indeed was a normal part of male culture at this time and beyond.

Talking about sex with your friends is an integral part of being a teenager. I have such fond memories of sleepovers where my friends and I would all share our own sexual snippets. We'd tell stories that we'd heard from older sisters or cousins, and once passed around a copy of Cosmopolitan magazine that someone had nicked from the doctor's office. I felt like I learned so much from those conversations, and I felt safe asking my friend's advice if there was something I was unsure about. When we actually began dating, it was a given that the more experienced friends would tell us all about their adventures. Rehashing the stories of your sexual adventures was a vital part of the whole experience. I was one of the last members of my friendship group to lose my virginity, and I felt so supported by them during that experience. When I was watching these movies, those scenes of friends talking about sex reminded me so strongly of my own experiences. If anything, I feel like this particular aspect of sexuality is so well captured by the teen movies from the 90's and 2000's. They paint such a clear picture of the importance of the peer group in learning about sex and sharing sexual experiences as a teenager.

Chapter 3

Masturbation

"It's like practice for The Big Game",- American Pie.

One can hardly talk about teenage sexuality without touching on the topic of masturbation. For many teenagers, the raging hormones of puberty, combined with newfound physical attractions to their peers often open the door to masturbation. For some, masturbation is a way to get to know their body as it changes, for some it can be a way to relieve sexual tension, and for others it's a way to practice for sex. Whatever the reason, masturbation is very common among teenagers, with up to 80% of boys and 48% of girls between the ages of 14-17 self-reporting that they regularly masturbate.[26]

Historically, masturbation was seen as a harmful practice, something that could be damaging to your physical health or a cause for shame. By the middle of the 20th century, attitudes towards masturbation

---

[26] Fortenberry et. al. (2010).

began to shift, and it became more accepted as a normal part of human sexuality.[27] By the nineties, there was still a fair amount of shame around masturbation, but it was generally viewed as a fairly normal and healthy way to express your sexuality. The teen movies of this time offer a snapshot of the attitudes surrounding the topic of masturbation.

A normal part of sexuality

When I was growing up, masturbation was something that was shrouded in secrecy. I caught mentions of it in books about puberty, magazine articles and occasional adult jokes. My first encounter with the word "masturbation" was in a book about puberty that my parents gave me. The book had entire chapters about menstruation and wet dreams that went into a lot of detail on these topics. On the topic of masturbation, there was a only a short paragraph that mysteriously alluded to it being something that a lot of young people do, that it feels really good and it's perfectly Ok to do it in private. But there was no definition of masturbation other than "touching your

---

[27] Greydanus and Omar (2014).

body in a way that feels good". I vividly recall being deeply confused about what that meant. There were lots of ways that I touched my body which felt good: running my hairbrush along my scalp, massaging my sore calves after rollerblading, scratching the rough skin on my knees. Was this masturbating? Should I only be doing these things in private? It took many years for me to piece together snippets of information from friends, magazines and scenes in movies to understand that no, none of these examples counted as masturbation.

I was very much brought up to believe that masturbation was something that everyone does, but nobody talks about. There's a scene in Mallrats which I feel perfectly illustrates the attitudes towards masturbation at the time. The protagonist, Brodie, tells a story about his cousin, Walter, who was on a plane that began to nosedive. Sensing that death was imminent, Walter pulls out his penis and begins furiously masturbating. Taking his cue, the other passengers also begin masturbating. Then the plane mysteriously rights itself and everyone puts their genitals away and deboards, never to speak of the event again. (Although clearly Walter did, because how else would Brodie have known about it?) This scene paints a picture that masturbation is great, so great that a whole plane full of people would be happy for it to be their final act. And in spite of how great it is, despite the fact that everyone was doing it, none of them would speak about it publicly. When a spellbound listener asks Brodie to go into more detail, he responds "Jeez! There's some things you just don't talk about!". To me, this scene perfectly sums up the general feeling about masturbation I grew up with – It's normal, it's great and we all do it. Just don't talk about it and for goodness sake, don't ask any questions about it!

Masturbation is a perfectly normal part of exploring your sexuality. And there are plenty of examples of adult characters in movies telling younger characters that jerking off is natural and widespread. In American Pie, after catching his son masturbating, Jim's father reassures him that it's perfectly normal and most people do it. 80's icon Molly Ringwald makes an appearance in Not Another Teen Movie to tell the protagonist that masturbation is healthy. Teen movies of the nineties and 2000's began to introduce representations of masturbation that had never been seen before on the big screen. The teenagers watching at home began to see that not only are lots of people are doing it, but lots of people are talking about masturbation and making movies about it too.

Masturbation- shameful or point of pride?

More often than not, the representations of masturbation in 90's teen movies are focused on young men. These representations show a dichotomous attitude towards masturbation. On the one hand, we see masturbation as something embarrassing: the earmark of a loser. On the other, we see it as a badge of honour and point of pride.

On one side of the coin, masturbation is depicted as something to be ashamed of. We see numerous characters hiding their masturbatory habits and feeling mortified at the notion that anyone would know that they enjoy jerking off. Sometimes, the fact that a character masturbates is used as shorthand to show that they are a nerd or a geek, someone who is unpopular. In Road Trip, the character Kyle is often made fun of for his regular masturbation. When his friends come to his room to ask a favour, he takes a long time to answer the door and they joke that it's probably because he was touching himself. In Just Friends, the protagnonist's nerdy younger brother is a virgin who admits to masturbating up to eight times a day. In these movies, masturbation is seen as something of a bad habit, something that you would only do if you couldn't get someone to have sex with you. It's implied that only losers masturbate and that regularly touching yourself is something to be ashamed of.

On the other side, there are numerous examples where a male character's masturbatory habits are a point of pride. In The Basketball Diaries, the protagonist and his friend have a competition to see who can jerk off the greatest number of times in a single day. In Kicking and Screaming, the main character's all-male friendship group regularly check in with one another to find out who has masturbated that day. Scenes such as these show masturbation as a kind of male bonding experience, something to talk about with your mates and not something to be ashamed of or hide. There is a degree of openness about masturbation between male friends in these movies.

I believe that these types of scenes are a pretty accurate representation of young men's masturbatory experiences. Although I couldn't find a lot of research on the topics, anecdotal reports from my male friends would suggest that it's fairly commonplace for teenage boys to discuss masturbation with their friends. I know many men who, as teenagers, talked at length with their friends about jerking off. Most of them have told me stories about watching pilfered pornography with their mates, and all touching themselves in the same room. I've heard tales of group camping trips that featured nightly jerk-off sessions around the campfire, with competitions to see who could orgasm the fastest. On the other hand, my own experiences as a teenage girl were vastly different. If my friends did masturbate, it was always deeply private and something that was never, ever discussed. Although I certainly masturbated as a teenager, I can't recall ever talking about it with my girlfriends, even though we would discuss practically every other detail of our lives.

Although female masturbation is shown less frequently, there are still many examples of it in the movies of this period. Unlike the representations of male masturbation, female masturbation isn't often shown as a source of shame. If it is shown, it is usually to illustrate that a character is sexually liberated, that she's in control of her own sexuality and pleasure. In American Pie, the character Nadia is depicted as stunning and self-assured, a sexual goddess. Her status as a sex kitten is cemented when she is shown masturbating on Jim's bed while reading a pornography magazine. In the same movie, band geek Michelle is proud of the fact that she knows how to get herself off, and openly discusses her masturbatory preferences. This scene flips the script on the depictions of geeks being chronic masturbators, as Michelle is not only honest about the fact that she masturbates but is proud of it.

There are also a number of scenes where older or more experienced women teach their friends how to find pleasure through masturbation. Also in American Pie, the character Jessica is sexually experienced and acts as a kind of mentor to her virginal friend, offering sage advice to improve her sex lives. Jessica is horrified when she finds out that her best friend, Vicky, has never "double clicked her mouse" and has never had an orgasm. She encourages Vicky to give it a try in an effort to get her more excited about the possibility of having sex. In Road Trip, the female lead, Beth, laments the untrustworthiness of men while talking to an older woman on the bus. The woman tells her "There is hope, but it comes with batteries" and gives her a vibrator. Pleasantville turns this trope on its head, when teenager Jen teaches her adopted mother, Betty, that it's possible for her to experience pleasure without her husband. In a later scene Betty is shown masturbating in the bathtub. When she orgasms, her black-and-white world is tinged with colour for the first time, visually representing the transformation and liberation that she has experienced. She is seeing the world through new eyes, seeing colours she never saw before.

These scenes differ starkly from my personal experience with masturbation as a young woman, as it was something that was very rarely discussed with friends. In high school, although I would discuss partnered sexual experiences in great detail with my female friends, we never talked about touching ourselves. However, by the time I got to university, it was a lot more common to talk about masturbation with my female friends. On several occasions I went shopping for vibrators with my mates and we were less embarrassed about talking about self-pleasure. This willingness to discuss this area of our sexuality may be explained by an increase in sexual confidence through experience, greater independence and a greater acceptance of female sexuality in media. By the time I got to university, all of the films discussed above had been released and I'd watched them a number of times. It was also the era of Sex and The City, which openly talked about masturbation and self-pleasure. I truly believe that these depictions of women being confident about touching themselves talking about it with their friends paved the way for many young women feeling less shame about their own masturbatory habits.

Masturbation as a placeholder for partnered sex

One of the reasons that masturbation can be such a healthy practice for teenagers is that it's a fantastic way to prepare for sex with a partner. Exploring your own body is a safe way to get to know your likes and dislikes, so that when you do begin having sex with someone else, you can communicate those preferences. It's a pressure-free way to start enjoying the pleasure that can be experienced through sex and it can be a valuable learning tool. In American Pie, Jim's father likens masturbation to being "practice for the big game". He then tells Jim that it can be fun on it's own, but ultimately seems relieved when Jim tells him that he would eventually like a partner to enjoy sex with.

This leads into another common trope that's shown in a lot of teen movies- the idea that masturbation is just a placeholder for partnered sex. A lot of films paint masturbation as a kind of watered-down version of sex, the thing you do until you can get The Real Thing. This depiction of self-exploration really diminishes the importance and value of masturbation as a sex act in and of itself. We see a lot of characters, usually male characters, who are using masturbation as a place

55

holder until they can secure a partner to begin exploring with. In Dead Man on Campus, the protagonist's roommate is a virgin who masturbates constantly. That is, until he meets a girl and falls in love, and the two of them begin having regular sex together. For this character, masturbation is a way to fulfill his sexual urges, and when he meets his girlfriend his sexual needs are fulfilled by their lovemaking. We often see depictions of young men who have not yet have partnered sex, but are using masturbation as a way to satisfy themselves until they find a willing partner.

There are also a number of depictions of young men who are sexually active, but for one reason or another are going through a sexual dry spell. These characters often turn back to masturbation as a means of relieving sexual tension until their sex lives are back on track. In Down to You, when the main character's girlfriend's anxiety puts a damper on their sex life, he begins masturbating a lot more frequently. Masturbation is regularly shown as something you do when sex isn't available.

Interestingly, despite the fact that there are numerous examples of female characters who enjoy masturbation, I can't find a depiction of a female character who replaces partnered sex with self pleasure. I can think of two reasons for this. The first is that in the fantasy world of movies, it is never difficult for a young women to find someone to have sex with. Women are usually depicted as sexual objects and are more likely to be shown trying to avoid having sex rather than searching for a way to attract a sexual partner. Therefore, if a young woman isn't having sex, it's usually because she's chosen not to. Secondly, there's a common attitude that women are better at controlling their sexual urges than young men. Many people believe that young boys are more sexually-driven and struggle to control their impulses. Whether or not this is true is debatable, but this idea of teenage boys as being led by their penises in most matters is frequently seen in teen moves of this period. On the flipside, young women are rarely shown to have sexual desires of their own, independent of the urges of their male counterparts. If young women are believed to have fewer sexual desires and are better at suppressing their urges than young men, then it makes sense that they are less frequently depicted as needing to resort to masturbation to curb their desires.

Common depictions of masturbation in film

One thing I find particularly interesting is the depictions of masturbation practices in these films. Occasionally, the characters do more than just talk about how the pleasure themselves, and we actually get a scene that shows their masturbation preferences. The reason I find these scenes interesting is that, as we've established, young people often seek sex education from television and films. Not only may these scenes reflect the actual practices of real-life teenagers (or be based on real life experiences of the writers) but it's possible that these scenes may inform the way that teenagers choose to explore their own sexuality. If they view a scene where a character masturbates, then it's possible that this scene may germinate an idea in the mind of the viewer about what might feel good, and they may emulate the scene. In some cases, that could be beneficial, and in others disastrous depending on the scene and film.

58

Pornography often plays a large role in masturbation scenes in films from the 90's and 2000s. This is hardly surprising when one considers that a large number of pre-teen and teenage boys have watched pornography.[28] In American Pie, Jim attempts to hack into the cable box so that he can watch an illegal adult channel while he masturbates. In the sequel, American Pie 2, Jim is gifted a pornographic movie on VHS by a friend. In 40 Days and 40 Nights, the protagonist clears away a large crate of pornographic material when he makes a Lenten pact to give up masturbation.

Lubrication is an oft-underutilized tool when it comes to sex and masturbation. There can stigma around using lubricant, particularly when a vagina is involved. There's a misconception that if a person with a vagina is enjoying themselves, they will automatically become wet. Of course, there are many reasons why a vagina may not self-lubricate even if it's owner is having a great time, such as alcohol, hormonal imbalances,

---

[28] Greydanus & Omar (2014).

anxiety and a host of other factors. Lack of lubrication may also be seen as an issue that more commonly impacts older vaginas, and therefore may be left out of the conversation about teenage sex. This is a huge shame, because store-bought lubrication can make sex and masturbation a great deal more comfortable and pleasurable regardless of the gender of the person using it. I found only two mentions of lubrication in relation to masturbation. Earlier I mentioned the crate of porn that gets packed away in 40 Days and 40 Nights, and along with that crate is a large tub of Crisco vegetable shortening. The implication is that the grease is being used as lubricant for masturbation. Many young men will use products like coconut oil, petroleum jelly or vegetable shortening as lubrication for masturbating because they're readily available from the pantry or bathroom cupboard and they don't have to go through the embarrassment of purchasing or hiding lubricant. In American Pie 2, Stifler gifts each of his friends a pornographic video and a tube of water-based lubricant. When Jim asks him, "Does it really make a difference?" Stifler replies in the affirmative. Lubricant reduces friction and can make masturbating a penis more comfortable and more pleasurable. Scenes like this one can help to break down the stigma around purchasing and using lube, and hopefully will encourage more pleasure and exploration among viewers.

Another object that can enhance sexual exploration is sex toys. Sex toys come in more varieties than I can list here, and they can be a valuable tool in getting to know your own body and learning to give yourself pleasure. Sex toys are only rarely shown in teen movies, and usually only in scenes that feature young women masturbating. In Not Another Teen Movie, Laney is shown using a large, gyrating vibrator with flowers painted on it. As mentioned earlier, Road Trip contains a scene where the female lead is gifted a slim, battery-operated vibrator. But I'm A Cheerleader features a scene with a young woman masturbating using an electric taser. Sex toys are usually only shown to be used by young women. If a young man is shown using something other than his hand to masturbate, it's usually a household object. The most well-known example of this is Jim having sex with an apple pie in American Pie. There are also instances of

61

young women using objects other than purpose-made toys to pleasure themselves, such as American Pie's Michelle admitting to using her flute to get herself off.

As I mentioned previously, during my own adolescence I struggled to find even a definition of masturbation, let alone detailed information about how to do it. Sex education books glossed over masturbation and rarely even talked about which body parts might be involved, let alone specific techniques. When a movie talked about masturbation, or actually showed someone doing it, I grabbed onto that information with both hands. It was frustrating for me when most of the scenes about masturbation centred around young men, and teenage girls were rarely shown to masturbate. American Pie was a turning point for me, because it features at least three female characters talking about how they like to touch themselves or masturbating on screen. I feel like American Pie demystified female masturbation for me a little and emboldened me to try new ways to explore my own body. (Although no baked goods were ever involved).

I have mixed feelings about the depictions of masturbation in the teen movies from the 1990's and 2000's, because although they are accurate in many ways, I feel like they paint a picture of sexual openness and confidence that simply wasn't there during my teen years. I feel like a lot of the characters in these films are much more self-aware of their own sexual needs, and a lot more comfortable talking about them than I would have been at the same age. Particularly for young women during this time, the attitude was definitely "everyone does it, nobody talks about it" but these films paint a picture of everyone doing it and talking about it. Although this might not be an accurate snapshot of the social norms of the time, I don't think that's a bad thing. As I mentioned earlier, seeing characters on the screen exploring their sexuality and talking about it emboldened me to do the same. Normalizing masturbation through positive depictions in film reduces the shame around what is a very common and natural sexual practice, and allows more people to feel OK about exploring their body and discussing it with their friends. Although films are not intended to be educational tools, they can certainly play a part in influencing social norms and inviting conversation about topics that had been previously shrouded in shame. And I feel like that happened during this period regarding the stigma around masturbation.

Chapter 4

The Impact of Peer Pressure

"It says here that 92% of honeys at UCLA are sexually active...You know what that means? It means I got a 92% chance of embarrassing myself", Can't Hardly Wait.

Something that has stuck in my mind about my pre-teen years was how often the topic of peer pressure was brought up. Parents and teachers alike were incessantly warning about the dangers of peer pressure. My grade six class was made to watch a video about peer pressure, in which a "good" girl was coerced by the popular kids into shoplifting so that she could join their group. My parents started talking a lot more frequently about how important it was to "do the right thing" and "follow your conscience" rather than doing what everyone else was doing. It seemed like everyone anticipated that once I started high school, that the lures of peer pressure would start coming hard and fast.

In a way, they weren't wrong. In high school I felt a much stronger pressure to dress a particular way and follow certain social rituals. I was very aware that there was a prescribed way of doing things, and if you deviated from that, you were labelled "square", "weird" or "a freak". Conformity is the name of the game in adolescence, and there was no reward for standing out and doing your own thing.

When it comes to sex, peer pressure is an almighty force to be reckoned with. A 1998 study found that the most prevalent driving force behind teen sexual activity was peer pressure.[29] Teenagers are likely to start engaging in sexualized behaviour not necessarily because they want to or because they're ready to do so, but rather because they don't want to be left behind by their peers. A further study found that teenagers are 2.5 times more likely to have sex by the time they start 9th grade if they believe that their peers are having sex.[30] This is true regardless of whether their friends are *actually* having sex. This study also

---

[29] Kinsman et al. (1998).
[30] Calabia (2001).

showed that teenagers often overestimate how many of their peers are sexually active. So not only are teenagers heavily influenced by the perception that they will fall behind their peer if they don't have sex, but this pressure is based on a faulty assumption.

Pressure to "lose It"

Teen movies from the 90's and 2000's build upon the theme of feeling pressured to have sex so as not to fall behind. This conundrum usually comes to the fore in the context of having sex for the first time. The idea of "stigmatized virginity", or the belief that a person is socially inferior due to the fact that they're a virgin, can generate a great deal of anxiety for young people.[31] The pressure to "just get it over with" is high, especially for young men. Many young people view the loss of virginity as a rite of passage, with virginity being something to cast off as quickly as possible so as not to fall behind one's peers. The reasons for the stigma surrounding virginity are complex, but in a 2017 study, Corliss noted with interest that a number of her subjects cited films or television shows where

---

[31] Corliss (2017).

someone is rejected because they're a virgin as part of their belief that virginity is a social stumbling block.

There was a slew of movies that came out at the tail-end of the 1990's which centred around the quest to have sex before heading off to college. The most noteable of these films is, of course, American Pie. The entire plot of this film revolves around a group of four male friends who make a pact to lose their virginity before high school ends. The quartet are mortified at the idea that they might go to college as virgins and the protagonist, Jim, wails that "They probably have special dorms for people like us". Their quest is based on the idea that if they don't lose their virginity in high school, they'll be ridiculed when they get to college. As it is, they are already facing a lot of direct pressure in the form of their friend Stifler. Stifler is vastly more sexually experienced than they are and takes every opportunity to poke fun of them for their lack of success with the ladies.

Interestingly, the catalyst for the pact in American Pie is the moment where the four main characters witness the class nerd, Sherman, farewelling a beautiful woman that he has spent the night with. Sherman then confirms that he is no longer a virgin. The characters feel insecure that they might be lagging behind. The fact that even Sherman has surpassed them sexually causes them to panic and start a quest to lose their virginity before they head off to college.

Towards the climax of the film, it is revealed that Sherman has lied about losing his virginity. Following this revelation, the boys are visibly relieved that they haven't been sexually eclipsed by someone that they perceive as socially inferior to them. This takes a lot of the pressure off them, as the yardstick that they've been measuring themself against is removed.

The Sprint to Lose Your Virginity Before College trope is also explored in 1998's Can't Hardly Wait. In this film, Kenny decides to throw all his efforts into having sex for the first time at his High School Graduation party. Kenny confides to his friends that he is concerned about embarrassing himself in college because he's not sexually experienced. He's honest about the fact that he doesn't know what he's doing, and that he feels inadequate because he hasn't had sex. His quest to have sex seems to be mostly based on the assumption that everyone at college will be more sexually experienced than he is, and that he'll make a fool of himself.

Both of these films depict the pressure that young men feel around sex. There's a pressure not only to be having sex, but also to be good at it. American Pie focusses more on the desire not to be the last virgin standing, while Can't Hardly Wait looks more closely at fear of inadequacy and inexperience. In both films, the assumption is made that losing your virginity is a transformative experience. Kenny in particular seems to believe that if he could just have sex once, then that single experience will teach him all he needs to know about sex. As we see in the final acts of both films, at least half of the characters have awkward first experiences with sex. In reality, it is fairly typical for teens to have less-than-perfect first times. Sex isn't a "one-and-done" activity, where you do it once and then magically know how to do it. It takes practice and time and experimentation to learn what you like and become adept at pleasing a partner. Both films seem to acknowledge this, with the characters learning that their first time is just the first step, and that it'll be a while before they feel sexually competent.

Sexual frequency and "manliness"

There are a number of other examples that expand upon this pressure for young men to be sexually prolific and competent. Seann William Scott seems to have based the early part of his career on playing characters that impose this pressure on his peers. Following his role as Stifler in American Pie, he plays E.L. in Road Trip (2000), a character who spends the majority of his time antagonizing his friend Josh about his love life. Josh is in a long-distance relationship and E.L. repeatedly pressures him to have sex with other girls. The fact that Josh is choosing to remain faithful and isn't engaging in sexual experimentation flies in the face of E.L.'s belief that college is a time where guys should be having sex as often as possible. His taunts eventually turn to admiration when Josh does decide to have sex with a woman other than his long-term girlfriend. In reality, sexual risk-taking behaviour, such as having unprotected sex or engaging in sex with multiple partners, is more likely to take place when teens believe that their friends would find these risks acceptable.[32] In Road Trip, Josh would likely not have cheated on his girlfriend if he didn't feel pressure from his friends to do so. Peer pressure is dangerous not only because it can lead teens to do things that they aren't ready for, but it can place them in precarious situations if they engage in risky sexual behaviour because they believe that risk is the norm in their peer group.

Male abstinence is frequently a source of peer pressure and jeering. In 40 Days and 40 Nights, the protagonist, Mark, decides to give up sex for Lent. Throughout the course of the film there is a tremendous amount of pressure on him to break his fast. Although some of the pressure comes from internal temptation, the majority of it comes from his friends. At one point one of his friends tells him that it's natural for men to have a lot of sex, and that by

---

[32] Jones, Salazar & Crosby (2017).

deciding not to have sex, Mark is going against nature. This undermines Mark's personal autonomy over his own sexuality and suggests that by choosing not to have sex, he's doing something truly bizarre. The pressure and taunts do not abate until Mark has finished his Lenten vow. In She's All That, the male protagonist is teased by his friends because he hasn't had sex in a long time, and they suggest that this is the reason why his performance on the soccer field has declined. Societal norms place pressure on young men to have multiple sexual partners and frequent intercourse to display their virility and masculinity.[33] Whether it occurs by choice or circumstance, male abstinence is often a source of ridicule. It creates a strong sense of pressure for young men to avoid going long periods without sex, and implies that if they do then they're somehow betraying their masculinity.

Peer pressure and female protagonists

Peer pressure does occasionally come up in films that feature female protagonists. In 10 Things I Hate About You, Kat reveals that she lost her virginity before she

---

[33] Jones, Salazar & Crosby (2017).

was truly ready because she felt pressured to do so. She tells her sister "Everyone was doing it, so I did it", and then admits that afterwards she decided that she didn't want to do it again because she wasn't ready. Scream's protagonist, Sydney, gives in to pressure from her boyfriend to lose her virginity. In Sydney's case, the pressure comes less from her friends and more from her partner, who often whines about the fact that they haven't had sex yet, despite being a couple for two years.

Teenagers often use their friend's behaviour as a yardstick to measure whether they're "normal". It's fairly common for teens to emulate their friends, whether that's choosing to wear the same clothes, using the same slang terminology or enjoying the same television programs and music. They may also try to keep step with their friend's sexual exploits, even if they don't necessarily feel ready to be having sex yet. In Thirteen, teenagers Tracey and Evie pick up two boys and begin making out with them. Things with Evie and her partner begin moving more quickly, as she climbs onto his lap and removes her top.

Seeing this, Tracey hops onto her partner's lap and removes her shirt as well. For the rest of the scene, Tracey tries to keep step with Evie as things get hotter. This scene illustrates the ways that young people can feel pressured to keep up with their friend's sexual behaviour, even if they themselves aren't necessarily ready for that type of physical intimacy. This particular film imparts the message that Evie has led Tracey astray, and that Tracey would not done so many dangerous things were it not for Evie's influence.

In my own experience, I felt very little peer pressure from friends to engage in sexual behaviour as a teenager. Within my friendship group, we talked candidly about our sexual encounters but there was rarely a sense of pressure or need to keep up. Some of us were more experienced than the others, and as one of the less experienced friends I felt pretty supported by my mates to go at my own pace and do what felt right to me. Although I dated a lot in high school and enjoyed kissing and other lighter sexual activities, my virginity was something that was very important to me. I made up my mind in my early teens that I didn't want to have sex until I was in a stable relationship with someone I cared about. And I never really felt pressure from my friends to deviate from this. Likewise, I didn't feel the need to lecture my more sexually-precocious friends about their choices. I was happy to hear about and learn from their experiences and they were happy to share with me. There was very little sexual peer pressure within my own friendship group.

For me personally, I felt the most pressure to engage in sexual behaviours from the boys I was dating. Whether it was a disappointed look when I told them I didn't want to go any further, an accusation that I was going to give them "blue balls" or outward wheedling to try to convince me to put out, I felt a tremendous amount of pressure from the people I was going out with. I also felt this same pressure from their male friends, who would make snide comments to me and ask when I was going to "give it up" to their friend. My personal experiences certainly mirror the scenes that I saw in the movies I watched as research for this book. The peer pressure came almost exclusively from boys, and I felt that the boys I dated were feeling inadequate and wanting to keep up with the perceived sex lives of their friends. I definitely felt like by not agreeing to have sex or engage in sexualised behaviours, I was somehow holding them back and making them feel like a loser amoung their friends.

When peer pressure did come from other girls, it was aimed in the opposite direction. More often than not, girls I knew would be shamed for having sex (or being perceived to have had sex). It was a lot more common to see girls being called a "slut" for having let a boy touch her breasts behind the shelter sheds or for making out with a boy at a party than it was to see girls pressuring one another to keep up sexually. I talk a lot more about "slut shaming" in the chapter about virginity, and in my experience peer pressure from other girls centered around not having sex.

Peer pressure is a significant factor in determining when a teenager will begin experimenting with sex. For young men in particular, this pressure stems not only from a desire to fit in with their friends, but also from the idea that male sexuality is tightly tied to virility and social desirability. This pressure is certainly present in the teen films from the 90's and 2000's, particularly when it comes to the rite of passage that is losing your virginity.

Chapter 5
The Challenges of Virginity

"You're a virgin who can't drive", *Clueless*.

I knew that when I set out to write this book, the topic of virginity was bound to be something I honed in on. So many of the teen films I remember from my adolescent years had a strong focus on virginity, whether it was about a character losing their virginity, maintaining their virginity, or simply considering the possibility of first-time sex. A lot of the ideas I had about the importance of virginity came from the films that I watched during this time in my life.

For me personally, I found the loss of my virginity fraught with difficulty. I held very conflicted ideas about what it meant to be a virgin. I believed that it was best to hold onto your virginity for as long as possible or until you'd met someone that you truly cared about. At the same time, I felt ashamed of my virginity on occasion, wishing that I was more

79

experienced and hoping to project an air of someone who was sexually confident. I wanted to appear sexually liberated well before I felt ready to actually have sex. When I did begin to question whether I was ready to have sex for the first time, I vividly remember thinking about specific scenes from teen movies I'd watched over and over, considering the stories that I was familiar with and comparing my own situation to them. I used these movies as a yardstick to measure my own readiness and weigh my options. So many of the values I held about losing my virginity were wrapped up in the stories I'd watched in teen movies from the 90's and early 2000's. It was interesting for me to go back and revisit these movies and begin to pick apart where some of those ideas and feelings began to take shape for me personally, as well as for my peers who grew up watching the same films.

What is virginity anyway?

Defining virginity is a very tricky business. There is no single agreed-upon definition, and people may define virginity as anything from complete innocence in matters of physical intimacy all the way through to someone who has done everything but sexual intercourse.[34] It is difficult to pin a definitive definition on a concept that is often only understood by its absence or loss.[35] Furthermore, a lot of the time our idea of what virginity is changes as we get older. This may occur as we learn more about sexuality and the sheer breadth of sexual acts (for example, someone may begin thinking of "virginity" as being someone who has never had sex with someone, but when they come to learn about oral sex, they may change their personal definition of virginity to be "someone who has never had penis-in-vagina sex"). The alteration of our definition of virginity may also take place as we become more sexually experienced, but still wish to consider ourselves "virgins" for one reason or another. Virginity may become more technical and nuanced.

Furthermore, it's important to consider that definitions of virginity that focus on penis-in-vagina sex may not apply for people who don't identify as heterosexual. Someone who identifies as a lesbian

---

[34] Jeffers (2005).
[35] Corliss (2017)

might have oral and manual sex with scores of female partners, but may still be technically considered a "virgin" because they've never had a penis in their vagina. Often, more traditional definitions of virginity are heteronormative and generate a very narrow idea of what "sex" is. When we consider sex as being any number of things that do not necessarily include a penis in a vagina, then the concept of virginity becomes even murkier.

One of my favourite scenes which discusses the topic of virginity at length takes place in Chasing Amy. In this scene the protagonist, Holden, discusses the idea of virginity and the definition of "sex" with his new friend Alyssa. Alyssa is a lesbian, although she has had intercourse with men in the past. Holden is very dismissive of the idea that lesbian sex - whether oral, manual or with a strap-on dildo - actually constitutes "real" sex. Alyssa scoffs at the notion and points out that lesbian sex is just as valid as penis-in-vagina sex. Alyssa defines the loss of virginity as "when you make love to a person for the first time", without putting a label on what that might entail. Holden then revises his definition to a more anatomically-based idea, that virginity is lost when the hymen is broken. Alyssa points out that many women have their hymen broken by means other than intercourse, so it's not a reliable measure of whether someone is a virgin or not. This scene beautifully highlights the difficulty of defining virginity: that one can take a purely physical standpoint (which doesn't apply to anyone whose sexual experience falls outside the heteronormative ideal of what sex should look like) or you can take a more open-minded and self-defined approach to deciding what virginity looks like (a person is no longer a virgin when they no longer feel like a virgin). Watching this scene for the first time was a turning point for me personally, because it completely questioned what I felt virginity was at the time and opened my mind to the possibility that virginity doesn't have a single definition and can mean many different things to different people.

When a concept has such a nebulous definition, there will always be exceptions and technicalities. The idea of the "technical virgin" is one that pops up frequently in films. The Technical Virgin is a character (usually a female character) who has learned to pay out lesser intimacies to a partner, without succumbing to full intercourse or loss of her innocence.[36] The Technical Virgin is someone who has done "everything but..." and still considers themselves to be a virgin despite their sexual experience. The best example of this concept is that of Dionne in Clueless. Early in the film, Dionne tells her friends that "My man is satisfied, he has no cause for complaints. But technically, I am a virgin". While she doesn't elaborate, the implication is that Dionne satisfies her boyfriend's sexual needs with acts other than intercourse, perhaps oral or manual sex. As the film progresses, and Dionne and her boyfriend grow closer, her best friend notes that "Dionne's virginity went from technical to non-existent", suggesting that Dionne and Murray have now begun having intercourse. The idea of Technical Virginity supposes two ideas. Firstly, that there is a hierarchy of sexual acts, with some having more weight or value than others (with penis-in-vagina sex being the top of the list). Secondly, that holding onto

---

[36] Jeffers (2005).

one's virginity is preferable but that there are other things you can do in the meantime to stave off having to submit fully. Interestingly, the concept of technical virginity also highlights that sexual expression can be divorced from desire, that a person can strategically permit certain acts but restrain themselves from others, even if they really do want to go all the way.[37]

Virgin Pride- maintaining virginity and maintaining status

Why would someone want to maintain their virginity? What is the purpose of continuing to claim the title of "Virgin" despite the fact that a person wants to enjoy sex and perhaps has some sexual experience? The reasons for this are incredibly complicated.

Firstly, it's very important to consider that virginity as a marker of status is gendered. Both in the films I studied, as well as in the wider population, the idea that virginity is something to be preserved applies most strongly to young women. Historically, virginity has impacted women much more heavily than it has

---

[37] Jeffers (2005).

men. In many cultures and societies, a woman's worth was based on her virginity, and being able to prove your virginity at the time of marriage was paramount. Establishing a woman's virginity not only ensured her virtuous character, but it had the practical implication of guaranteeing that any children she conceived were fathered by her husband. This was particularly important in patriarchal societies, where property and titles were passed through the family line, and nobody wanted an imposter to inherit family wealth. Serious consequences were faced by women who had sex before marriage, and it could impact the course of your entire life. The hymen has long been seen as a physical marker of virginity and purity, even though we know that this is not a reliable measure of whether or not a person with a vagina has had sex. There are many sexual acts that can be enjoyed without tearing the hymen, and conversely there are countless non-sexual acts that may result in damage to the hymen. There is no analogous physical marker on a male-bodied person that is supposed to indicate whether or not he has had sex. Similarly, young men have not faced the same backlash as young women in the past for having premarital sex. This historical context is important, because it flows through to present day.

The idea that maintaining "purity" by not having sex before marriage is still upheld in many communities and cultures today. In many religious communities, Purity Culture places a huge weight on young women to remain virgins until they're married. In communities that adhere to the idea that chastity is a marker of good character, a massive amount of ridicule is directed towards people who have sex prior to marriage. Similarly, in places where abstinence-only sex education is taught in schools, there is an unspoken message that shames students who may already have had intercourse.[38] Slut-shaming, the derogatory treatment of a woman for being sexual for the purpose of making her feel guilty or inferior, is common. Even though often, the sex act features both a boy and a girl, it is the girl who faces judgement and ridicule when her actions are made public.[39]

---

[38] Norwick (2016).
[39] Poole (2014).

Slut shaming is seen in many of the movies that I watched for my research. It is common to see a young female character who has had sex being ridiculed or excluded because of her sexuality. Interestingly, the character doesn't actually have to have had sex. Sometimes it's enough for them to behave in a suggestive manner or for their peers to merely believe that they have had sex. In Bring it On, the cheerleaders are disgusted by a character who performs a striptease as part of her cheerleading audition. Earlier in the film, the cheerleaders in their skimpy outfits chant lines such as "You can look, but don't you hump" and "I'm major, I roar, I swear I'm not a whore!". The contradiction between the cheerleader's behaviour and their rejection of an openly-sexual peer is strong. The idea this story presents is that it's ok to appear sexy and flirty, but it's not Ok to actually be sexual. There's a very fine line being drawn here between the acceptable presentation of sexuality and going too far and appearing slutty.

In Cruel Intentions, there are two characters who are virgins: Annette and Cecile. Annette is proud of her virginity and publicly publishes a "Virgin's Manifesto" detailing all the reasons why she intends to remain a virgin until she's married. The male lead, Sebastian, sets himself the goal of sleeping with Annette. He believes that it will be a conquest, a status symbol to seduce such a high-profile virgin. On the other hand, Sebastian's step-sister, Kathryn, enlists Sebastians help by asking him to sleep with Cecile to ruin her reputation. Kathryn knows that if Cecile is no longer a virgin, then she will be seen as "damaged goods". Kathryn is very sexually experienced and expresses her frustration that she enjoys sex, but has to hide her dalliances in order to be taken seriously. She considers it deeply unfair that men still prefer innocents and virgins over a more experienced and confident partner. This film presents an interesting look at the dichotomy between the virgin and the whore, and the status that is placed on virginity for women.

The idea of virginity as a commodity is also seen in 10 Things I Hate About You. In this film, popular jerk Joey pursues Bianca and goes to great lengths to secure her affections. He even makes a bet with his friends that he can sleep with her on prom night. As the film progresses, we learn that the main reason that Joey is interested in Bianca is that she is a virgin. Once again, we see the idea of the idealized virgin, a young woman who is seen as a prize mainly due to the fact that she is pure and untouched. Virginity is almost fetishized in this sense; it's seen as a sexually-attractive quality and something that draws men to pursue young women. Ironically, the very thing that they are attracted to will be gone the moment they succeed in their quest to bed her.

Virgin shaming

The flipside to virgin pride is Virgin Shaming. Virgin Shaming is based on the supposition that virginity is not a desirable attribute. There's an idea that someone who is a virgin is immature or unattractive; virginity can be seen as a marker of low social status in a culture that values sexuality. Although virginity stigma is something that has been historically related to young boys, as sexual expression in women becomes more socially acceptable, it has begun to impact young women more strongly.[40] Young people

---

[40] Corliss (2017).

may feel pressured to have sex in order to shake off the stigmatized label of "virgin", and this is something that we see presented in the teen movies of the 90's and 2000's.

I've touched on this topic already in the chapter regarding peer pressure. In this chapter, I talked at length about films in which young men feel pressured by perceived societal norms to lose their virginity before going to college. Films such as American Pie and Can't Hardly Wait tell the stories of young men who are anxious to have sex before high school ends, for fear of going to college a virgin. In her 2017 study, Aja Renee Corliss stated that many of her participants felt pressure to lose their virginity by the time they reached a certain age, or before they went to college. The end of high school seems to be a common arbitrary expiry date for virginity, with many young people feeling as though going to college as a virgin would bring shame and ridicule.

There are many other film examples of young people who are teased or looked down upon for being virgins.

In Crossroads, the character of Lucy is teased by her peers for being a virgin. In Van Wilder, college student Taj is mortified at the idea that he might have to return home after his freshman year without losing his virginity. In Teaching Mrs Tingle, the female protagonist Leanne is teased for being a virgin. There are many other examples of the 'loser" or "geek" character being teased for their virginity.

The 90's virginal depiction that I find the most interesting is that of Cher in Clueless. Cher is the most popular girl in school and she is also a virgin. Although she talks to her friends about her virginity and the fact that she wants to remain a virgin until she's found the right person to have sex with, not a lot is made of the fact that Cher's a virgin. None of the other characters draw attention to the fact that Cher isn't having sex, and her virginal status neither enhances nor hampers her popularity. However, at the climax of the film when Cher is fighting with Tai, her virginity is suddenly used as a barb against her. Mid-argument, Tai flings out the insult "You're a virgin who can't drive", and the effect on Cher is instantaneous and devastating. Although until this point Cher has felt neither shame nor pride in her virginity, Tai knows that hurling it in Cher's face is a sure way to hurt her. In this moment, the word "virgin" means "failure, unwanted, unattractive" and you can see the pain on Cher's eyes as the insult lands. Cher's popularity has never been damaged by the fact that she hasn't had sex, but the shame of virginity is still present and able to be weaponized against her.

The Virgin/ Slut paradox

When it comes to women, there is a definite push-and-pull at play around virginity. The line between "virgin" and "whore' is perilously thin, and as we've seen there are negative aspects to falling on either side of this line. Women in particular face this social stigma paradox where they are condemned for being too sexual, and also for being not sexual enough.[41] Young women are held to an impossible double standard, where they are expected to be sexy, but not too sexy. This confounding dilemma creates a lot of uncertainty and anxiety around sex, imposing a pressure on girls to seem sexually available and attractive, but not be

---

[41] Corliss (2017).

seen to be submitting too easily, too frequently and compromising their "purity".[42]

This dichotomy plays out in a number of ways in the teen films of the 1990's and 2000's. Most frequently, we see within the same movie characters being teased for being a virgin, and then later in the movie different characters being shamed for being too slutty. In Bend it Like Beckham, Jess's friends make fun of her because she's a virgin, and in the same conversation they begin ribbing one another over the number of sexual partners they've each had. The idea is that it's not good to be a virgin and it's not ok to be a slut, but the space in between these two concepts is nebulous and difficult to navigate.

We can even see examples of the exact same character being shamed on both sides of the paradox. In It's a Boy Girl Thing, Nell is teased mercilessly for being a virgin. Later in the film, a male character tells everyone that he and Nell slept together and she is then ridiculed for being a slut. Even though she hasn't actually had sex, the mere perception that she

---

[42] Poole (2014).

submitted and lost her virginity is enough to turn the tide on what she's being shamed for. This film shows the lose-lose situation that many young girls face with regards to their sexuality, that it doesn't really matter if they're having sex or not, they will be excluded and mocked regardless.

Getting it right the first time

There seems to be a lot of pressure not only about when you lose your virginity, but also how you lose it and who you lose it to. There's a distinct impression that there's a "right" and a "wrong" way to lose your virginity. The way a person feels about losing their virginity is tightly tied to their values around virginity and sex. For those who believe that having sex for the first time is important and that virginity is precious, then choosing the right partner and situation becomes vital. For a person who believes that their first time is special, then losing their virginity in less-than-ideal circumstances to a person who doesn't accept this gift in the desired way can damage their self-esteem.[43] On the other hand, if you hold the belief that losing your

---

[43] Corliss (2017).

virginity is just a rite of passage, something that everyone goes through eventually, then there may be less pressure for the circumstances surrounding your first time to be just right.[44]

The teen films of the 1990's and 2000's offer many narratives for this idea, both that it's important to choose the right person and situation to lose your virginity, and that failing to do so may have dire consequences. We also see many depictions of the anxiety and internal conflict that can arise from trying to make this decision.

American Pie offers one of the richest examples of this type of decision making. Although most of the main characters are virgins, it is through the character of Vicky that we see the strain and confusion as she decides how to lose her virginity. Vicky is in a committed, long-term relationship and she has expressed a desire to have sex with her boyfriend, Kevin. It is very important to Vicky that her first time is "perfect". Even though she and Kevin have many opportunities to have sex, she declines each time

[44] Corliss (2017).

because it doesn't feel right. Eventually, after many long discussions with her best friend, Vicky comes to the realization that if she wants the sex to be perfect, she's going to have to make it perfect. So, she makes a plan to have sex with Kevin for the first time on prom night. When the night comes, Kevin secures a private, romantic room at a friend's house and they set out candles. They undress and get into bed together, but from that point on their encounter is somewhat stiff. We see them lying in bed next to one another, not touching, deciding what position to have sex in. Each time the camera cuts to the couple, they're awkwardly touching one another, avoiding eye contact even in the moment when they are actually having sex. Afterwards we see them getting dressed on opposite sides of the room. Even though the situation was "perfect" the sex itself feels stilted and stiff, almost like an interaction between strangers rather than a couple who have been dating for years.

On the other hand, we see a contrasting sex scene between Heather and Oz, who have been casually dating for a few weeks. This couple hadn't planned on having sex ahead of time, but when Oz asks Heather if she wants to, she agrees. They go to a private boathouse, and we see them kissing and caressing each other. The soft camera work gives the impression that a lot of time is passing, that they're just enjoying being with one another and exploring. We see them undress one another and the whole thing feels very unhurried and relaxed. The morning-after shot of the two of them is very intimate and it creates a completely different feeling to the scene with Kevin and Vicky. American Pie seems to give the impression that while you can plan the perfect time to lose your virginity, you can't plan chemistry and spontaneity, and sometimes it's best to just go with the flow.

In Looking for Alibrandi, the protagonist, Josie, spends a lot of her time thinking about sex and the right time to lose her virginity. Josie is a perfectionist, and she feels a lot of pressure to do things "just right". Add to the mix her Catholic upbringing and you have a young woman who is fixated on not making a misstep with her virginity. Josie is exploring a relationship with Jacob, who has a more relaxed attitude to sex and has had sex with other girls. In one scene, we see Josie visit Jacob at home. When he leads her to his bedroom things quickly heat up. They begin kissing and Jacob starts to climb on top of her. Josie stops him, and they cool off a little and then things resume. As he begins to put his hand up her skirt, Josies once again tells him to stop because it doesn't feel right. Josie is torn between enjoying the physical exploration with Jacob, and wanting her first time to be "just right". Jacob becomes angry and asks Josie "what is it, a prize?" implying that she doesn't think he's good enough for her. Josie leaves feeling angry and confused, but relieved that she didn't give in and lose her virginity in circumstances that didn't feel right to her.

Another example where reality and expectation do not meet is in 1995's Empire Records. In this film, Corey is a virgin and a perfectionist. She has made the decision to lose her virginity to Rex Manning, an ageing rock star who is visiting the record store where she works. Corey plans every detail of the encounter and arranges to be the one to bring Rex his lunch so that she can seduce him. Her plans go awry when Rex doesn't treat her gesture as something special and is flippant about the idea of them having sex. Realizing that she's made a mistake and that the encounter doesn't mean anything to him, Corey angrily leaves, pulling on her clothes as she exits the room in tears. This scene typifies the frustration and loss of self-esteem that may be felt if a prospective partner does not accept the "gift" of virginity with the reverence the virgin believes it deserves.

Interestingly, most of the films that show a character agonizing over the right time, place or partner for their first time usually focus on female characters. Although a male character might be seen to think about losing his virginity and planning for the first time they have sex, they often exhibit more excitement, and an eagerness to get it over with. There are several possible reasons for this. Firstly, as I mentioned earlier in this chapter, the very concept of virginity has historically been gendered, geared more towards females than males. Virginity is more likely to be seen as an asset to a young woman, and a liability to a young man. Secondly, young women in the real world feel more pressure than boys to get it right the first time, and are more likely to feel guilt or regret about the loss of their virginity than their male counterparts.[45]   Finally, it has been proposed that young men tend to be more excited about the first time that they have sex because it's more likely that it will be pleasurable for him.[46] For young men, first time sex has a high probability of being a pleasurable experience, and therefore something they're more excited and eager to experience. Young women are less likely to experience pleasure or climax during their first sexual experience, and first penetration can be an uncomfortable or even painful experience for a young woman. Only 11% of young women report having an orgasm the first time they have vaginal intercourse.[47] 52% of women report pain the first time they have sexual intercourse.[48]   In the scenes I've already discussed, it is unusual to see a young woman having an orgasm the first time she has sex.   In American Pie, for example, when Vicky is talking to Jessica about the first time, she asks if it's going to hurt and Vicky acknowledges that the first time is going to be painful. This is confirmed when, later in

---

[45] Lipman & Moore (2016).
[46] Delamater (1987).
[47] Higgens et al (2010).
[48] Higgens et al (2010).

the movie, we see Vicky gasp as Kevin penetrates her for the first time. Conversely, we do not see her experiencing pleasure the first time, and her experience seems more awkward and uncomfortable than exciting. There are many reasons why young women, both in film and in reality, might feel more trepidation around the loss of their virginity and therefore be more likely to plan the event with care.

In the real world, we see evidence that young women report more satisfactory first-time sex when they are in a committed relationship with their first sexual partner. While there are a number of reasons for this, one of the most significant seems to be that women who have sex for the first time with a partner they are committed to feel less guilt, as it is more socially acceptable to lose your virginity to a long-term partner than during a casual encounter. It may also be that women who wait for a steady partnership before having sex for the first time may feel more ready for sex and may be more in control of their first sexual experience, which in turn will lead to greater satisfaction in that experience.[49]

There are also depictions in film of young women who do not take the loss of their virginity seriously, and experience a downfall as a result of discarding their virginal status. In The Virgin Suicides, Lux Lisbon has sex with her homecoming date on the football field. The encounter is rushed and awkward, and afterwards he leaves her alone in her grass-stained dress to find her way home. After this, Lux is grounded by her parents and enters a period of depression and sexual promiscuity, inviting many random boys onto the roof of her house for a series of open-air affairs. The Lisbon family in this film are very religious and place a high value on purity. Lux's loss of virginity is painted as the misplacement of something precious, and the fact that she seems to have given it away with little thought or planning is shown to have disastrous consequences.

Loss of virginity and personal transformation

---

[49] Higgens et al (2010).

As the loss of one's virginity may be seen as a rite of passage or turning point for a character, it stands to reason that it is often shown as a transformative experience. Much like the common "makeover" scene, where a character emerges with a new look, we often see scenes where a character loses their virginity and is emotionally or socially transformed by the encounter.

One depiction of virginity loss that I find particularly interesting is in Road Trip. In this film, the character Kyle is a virgin and is often made fun of by his friends for this fact. During the gang's adventure, Kyle meets a young woman at a frat house and ends up having sex with her. Before they have sex, we see the pair lying in bed together as Kyle confesses that this is his first time. His partner isn't deterred by this and she tells him that she believes it's important that the first time is special. She takes the lead, telling Kyle where he can find condoms, helping him to put on a condom and finally climbing astride him. The thing that I find fascinating in this depiction is the before-and-after transformation of the character. In a paper by Jeffers (2005) looking at depictions of virginity in film, the author discusses the difficulty in how to portray a virgin on screen. She highlights the challenge of finding a way to visually represent an invisible quality, in a way that makes it recognizable that the character is sexually inexperienced. In films from the 1990's and 2000's, virgins are often depicted as being unfashionable and prudish. They often wear modest clothing, or clothing that is more suitable for a conservative adult rather than a carefree teenager. Their body language is often self-conscious, with a hunched posture, pigeon-toed stance and glance that rarely leaves the floor. When we see Kyle on screen during his introduction, he immediately looks awkward and shy. His clothes are too big for him, he seems ill-at-ease and he rarely meets the gaze of his friends. After he has sex for the first time, he emerges the next morning with his head held high, visibly more relaxed and with a swagger in his step. This scene shows a marked difference in Kyle, imparting the message that sex is transformative and that you'll be a different, better person after you lose your virginity. Losing your virginity is shown as a way to shrug your way out of teenage awkwardness and emerge confident and glowing.

Not all first-time transformations are positive though. To contrast the scene with Kyle, I want to look at the character of Kenny from Can't Hardly Wait. Kenny attends his graduation party with the sole purpose of losing his virginity. After many failed attempts, Kenny finds himself sleeping with Denise, a childhood friend that he has since drifted away from. Denise has had sex before, but only once. After they have sex, they are shown lying awkwardly on the floor of the bathroom where they've hooked up, not making eye contact and stiffly covering their bodies with a towel. As they get up and begin to dress, Denise makes the mistake of telling Kenny "It gets better, y'know, it can go for longer". His face instantly falls into a mask of shame and disappointment and he storms out. Kenny had hoped that losing his virginity would be transformative, that his first time would resolve all of his hang-ups and infuse him with confidence. Instead, it only seems to have cemented his fear that he has no idea what he's doing, and he leaves feeling worse than he did when the night began.

Virginity is a hugely complicated topic, and one that has been a fundamental part of many teen movies. The depictions of virginity and the ways that people who choose to protect or lose their virginity are treated by the other characters creates a narrative of what is normal and good. Watching these films as a teenager definitely informed my own ideas about sex, and I used the experiences depicted on the screen as a yardstick for how I should behave. I remember thinking about some of these scenes at the point in my life where I was considering having sex for the first time, and trying to measure myself against the characters to decide whether I was ready. I definitely internalized some of the messages about how much to submit, how important it was to seem sexually desirable and available but not too much. I know for a fact that a lot of my own anxiety around having sex for the first time was compounded by the fear of not doing it right, of not choosing the right time or the right partner. It is interesting to look back with the benefit of hindsight to begin to see where those seeds were planted, and which stories took root in my own mind as I was forming my own ideas about virginity.

Chapter 6
Contraception

"Well, what do you suggest I use?"
"How about your underpants?", Looking for Alibrandi

You would expect that the subject of sex and birth control would go hand-in-hand. When you consider a genre of movies that tends to discuss the subject of sex fairly frequently, it's surprising that the topic of birth control rarely makes an appearance. A 2014 study which looked at the relationship between television viewing and condom use found that only 5.2% of television episodes that showed sexual content featured any mention about taking contraceptive precautions.[50] When I began researching contraceptive use in teenagers, I was surprised by how few teenagers are actually using birth control. In a 2015 paper, it was reported that around 38% of grade 9-12 students who are having sexual intercourse did

---

[50] Mohamad. (2014).

not use proper protection.[51] The lack of birth control in the teen movies from the 90's and 2000's reflects the fact that many sexually active teenagers at this time were not using birth control.

If it's not on, it's not on

I did notice that when contraceptives are shown, there isn't a lot of variety in the type of methods that are depicted. By far, the condom is the most widely present form of birth control in the teen movies that I looked at when researching this book. In a way this makes sense, as condoms are probably the birth control method that most teenagers would be familiar with. Condoms are inexpensive, they're available for purchase at grocery stores, pharmacies, petrol stations and vending machines. Anyone can purchase them without the need to visit a doctor for a prescription, they're easy to hide and fairly simple to use. Most sex education programs that discuss contraception usually cover the use of condoms and many teenagers will feel familiar and somewhat comfortable with the humble condom. Condoms are

---

[51] Le Brun and Omar (2015).

also fairly widely promoted because of their use not only as a form of birth control, but also for their usefulness in protecting against sexually transmitted diseases. More often than not, when a teen movie shows contraceptives, it is usually a condom that is shown.

Another reason that condoms are likely to be shown most frequently is that they are easily recognizable to most teenagers. While many teenagers may never have seen a diaphragm or a package of contraceptive pills, most of them will have seen a condom at some point, and therefore the presence of a condom (either wrapped or unwrapped) quickly signals to the audience that the characters in the movie are going to have sex, and that they're using protection. Even if the characters never mention the condom, the mere fact that it's there shows that they're having protected sex. In movies such as 40 Days and 40 Nights, Road Trip and Van Wilder, condoms are shown either before or during sex scenes. In Crazy/Beautiful, the protagonist, Nicole, tiptoes to the medicine cabinet to retrieve a condom before taking her love interest, Carlos, by the hand and leading him to her room.

Without saying a single word, this single gesture shows both Carlos and the audience that Nicole intends to have sex with him. In Mean Girls, Regina's mother taps on the door and offers her a condom when she's in her room making out with a boy. Condoms are by far the most represented form of contraception in teen movies.

Condoms feature prominently in scenes that show sex education classes. In Never Been Kissed, the sex education class is instructed to put condoms onto bananas (even though the teacher points out that the bananas don't bear any real resemblance to actual genitalia). In a humorous twist on abstinence-only education, the sex education class in Mean Girls is told that if they have sex they will "get pregnant and die" before the teacher passes around condoms to the class. In Ginger Snaps, when the title character gets her first period, the school nurse hands her a pack of condoms and tells her that now that she's menstruating, she will need to protect herself from pregnancy and sexually transmitted diseases. Funnily enough, later in the film when Ginger does have sex, she does not heed this warning and fails to use any sort of protection. This scene illustrates the real-life fact that while a lot of teenagers are aware of the importance of birth control, many still resist using it for a variety of reasons.[52]

The symbolic significance of birth control

Many films show teenagers purchasing birth control in anticipation of their first sexual experience. Sometimes the character has a definite plan to have sex, with a particular person or event in mind. Other times, they may simply be acting on their hope that they will eventually get to have sex, even if the prospect is a remote one. In American Pie, we see Kevin purchasing condoms and distributing them to his friends in preparation for their quest to lose their respective virginities. In Mona Lisa Smile, Giselle proudly presents her friends with her newly-acquired diaphragm, to which her less-experienced friend Connie replies "Maybe I'll get one". Connie doesn't have a partner or even a love interest at this point in the story, but she's eager to be prepared just in case the opportunity arises. In Varsity Blues, Mox buys a

---

[52] Carvalho et al (2006).

box of condoms before his date with Darcy, as he hopes that they will have sex after they've been out together. In these cases, acquiring contraceptives is not only a preparatory act, but something that signals the characters readiness for sex. The condoms and diaphragm act as a totem, a symbol that the character is ready for sex, and prepared for it whenever it may happen.

This also recognizes that not having contraceptives at hand may be a barrier to sex if the character finds themselves in a situation with a partner who is ready and willing to have sex. In Boys and Girls, Jennifer tells her friends that she had planned to have sex with her date but the fact that neither one of them had a condom put a stop to it. In Kicking and Screaming, Grover's date is almost cut short when he and his partner find themselves without a condom, until her roommate finds one for them and they are able to continue having sex.

The presence of contraceptives not only signals that a teen is ready to have sex, but it may also act as a clue to their parents that their teenager is sexually active (or is planning to have sex in the near future). In the movie Fear, Nicole's father becomes irate after finding a condom wrapper under her bed. He confronts her and tells her that she's ruining her life by having sex. Nicole had attempted to hide her sexuality from her father, and the condom wrapper was the evidence that gave her away. In fact, many teenagers have said that the reason that they are hesitant to buy birth control is fear that their parents will find it and become upset with them.[4] For teens who feel that their parents wouldn't approve of them having sex, this can be a barrier to them keeping condoms or other contraceptives on hand. It doesn't make it less likely that they will have sex, only that they are less likely to use protection when they do. Parental disapproval and fear of their parents finding out can be a significant barrier to teenagers choosing to purchase birth control.

Going without...

Often, teenagers make the decision not to use birth control for a variety of reasons. Religious beliefs may prohibit contraceptive use (although interestingly most religions that disapprove of contraceptives also do not permit premarital sex). Teenagers may feel that contraceptives are difficult to obtain, may be unsure how to use them or may believe that they don't need to use birth control because they believe "it won't happen to me". We see a couple of examples of these types of attitudes in the films I studied. In Where the Heart Is, Novalie and her best friend never use birth control, despite the fact that both of them have had unplanned pregnancies in the past. At one point, Novalie has unprotected sex with a mechanic, and then prays that she will get her period. When her period arrives, she thanks God. This reliance on the "poke and pray" method is dangerous, particularly when we know that this character has experienced the consequences of unprotected sex before. In Looking for Alibrandi, Ana expresses concern over her friend Sarah's promiscuity and the fact that she's not using birth control. When Sarah asks her friends "well, what do you suggest I use?", the protagonist, Josie, retorts "How about your underpants?". This implies that Josie thinks that Sarah would be safer abstaining from sex, rather than having unprotected sex. While it's true that abstinence is the best form of protection against pregnancy and sexually transmitted diseases, there are plenty of effective contraceptive methods available for teenagers who choose to have sex.

Inconsistencies and misinformation

One of the concerns I had about the depictions of contraceptives in teen movies is the potential for dissemination of incorrect information about contraceptive use. As I've mentioned before, when teenagers are not given comprehensive sex education, they are likely to look to other sources for information about sex. If the sources where they seek answers to their questions are inaccurate, then they could be placing themselves in danger if they take the information they've gathered as gospel. I found a couple of examples of incorrect information about contraception in the movies that I watched. In American Pie, Michelle instructs Jim to wear two condoms when they have sex, to desensitize him so that he will last longer. In Can't Hardly Wait, Kenny decides to put on two condoms before heading out to hook up with a girl at a party because he doesn't know the girl. He seems to think that wearing two condoms at a time will offer him double the protection against STDs. In fact, wearing two condoms at once may actually decrease their effectiveness. The extra layer of latex can generate additional friction and wear, increasing the likelihood of both condoms breaking. It's also common to see characters carrying condoms in their wallets for extended periods, which is not recommended because of the danger of heat and friction degrading the latex. While these scenes exist for entertainment value, rather than to educate viewers about correct condom use, this misinformation could be potentially dangerous if viewed by a teenager who hasn't received proper education about contraceptives.

Another piece of misinformation is found in the movie Boys and Girls. In one scene, the character Jennifer says that she has her period, and that she could have sex right now and not get pregnant. It is a common misconception that a woman can't get pregnant while she's on her period. In fact, while it's much less likely for conception to occur if a woman has sex while she's menstruating, it isn't impossible. Factors such as the length of cycle, the number of days between menstruation and ovulation and the hardiness of the sperm can all play a part, and it is possible for a woman to get pregnant if she has sex during her period. As most teenagers tend to have irregular periods for the first few years, and few teenagers closely monitor their cycles and understand the different stages of the menstrual cycle, viewing menstruation as a "safe" time to have sex can be misleading and potentially disastrous.

Interestingly, contraceptives are often not shown in scenes where a character becomes pregnant or where a pregnancy scare occurs. This is reflective of statistics which show that the majority of teen pregnancies occur in couples who are not using any form of birth control. Although contraceptives can be used incorrectly or may fail, the movies I studied tended to leave out any discussion of contraceptives when the storyline focused on teen pregnancies. I discussed this concept in more detail in the chapter about teen pregnancy, but essentially when a character in a teen film falls pregnant, they are not usually shown to be using any kind of birth control.

Contraceptives are not often featured in teen movies, even when sex is one of the main plot points. When they are featured, it's most common to see easily-recognizable forms of contraceptives, such as condoms. Often, the presence of contraception in a scene is less about promoting the message of safer sex, but rather about communicating to the audience. A scene in which a character buys condoms indicates that they are hoping to have sex. The presence of a condom wrapper in a scene communicates to the audience that sex has taken place. Contraceptives are used as filmmaking shorthand to express the characters sexuality and sexual motives in movies that may not actually show them having sex. This is perfectly valid, as films are a form of storytelling, and aren't usually intended to educate the viewer. I don't find it concerning that so few films show contraception, but I was surprised at how infrequently it gets mentioned in a genre that discusses sex so often. What is concerning to me is the low levels of real-life contraceptive use among teenagers. The research in this area clearly shows a need for more education about contraception, and greater accessibility to contraception for teenagers, so that when they do begin having sex they can do so with a greater degree of safety.   The fact that perceived parental disapproval is cited as a significant barrier to contraceptive use suggests to me that parents have a role to play in teaching their children about safer sex practices and reducing stigma around contraceptive use.

Chapter 7

Teen Pregnancy

"Kissing isn't what keeps me up to my elbows in placenta all day long", 10 Things I Hate About You.

In the 1990's and early 2000's, the USA had the highest rate of teen births in the developed world.[53] Teen pregnancy is a huge issue of concern for teenagers who are beginning to explore their sexuality, and one of the most serious consequences of unprotected sex. It's unsurprising then that teen pregnancy is a common theme in movies aimed at teenagers. The late nineties and early 2000's saw a handful of films that featured teen pregnancy as a central plot point, and even more where it was raised in a more roundabout fashion. Movies such as Where the Heart Is, Saved and Riding in Cars with Boys centred on teenage girls dealing with the consequences of unplanned pregnancy.

Teen Pregnancy as a cautionary tale.

---

[53] Poynter (2014) 2.

A common thread that runs through most of the stories of teen mothers depicted in these films is the idea that if a teen girl falls pregnant, it will ruin her life. These movies depict teen pregnancy as a disaster, and something to be avoided at all costs.

When we look at the real-life consequences of teenage pregnancy, the outcomes are usually not positive, particularly for young mothers. Teen parents often obtain a lower level of education than their peers. The dropout rate for teens who become pregnant is about 40%, and most find it difficult to resume schooling once they have dropped out.[54] They tend to have more limited employment opportunities, and show a higher rate of substance abuse and illegal activity.[55] While there are certainly cases of teen parents who go on to obtain higher education and successful careers, the statistics show that these were few and far between, particularly in the 1990s when there were fewer opportunities for young parents. The general attitude has been that teenage pregnancy is something to be

---

[54] Carvalho Sant'anna et al (2006).
[55] Greydanus, Huff and Omar (2012). 392.

avoided, and that measures should be put in place to educate young people so that they can avoid unwanted pregnancy. [56]

It should be noted that in the films I studied, all of the teen pregnancies featured were unplanned. As around 82% of all teen pregnancies are unintended[57], it makes sense that the film depictions of teenage mothers almost exclusively feature unplanned pregnancies.

Several of the films I examined featured young female protagonists dealing with the consequences of an unwanted pregnancy. In these films, their pregnancy is often framed as an obstacle which must ultimately be overcome for them to achieve their dreams. We often see the trope of a promising young woman whose life is derailed when she becomes pregnant. In Dangerous Minds (1995) Callie has to give up her education when she finds out that she's pregnant. Although she is excelling at school and has just unearthed a passion for writing, her school refuses to

---

[56] Poynter (2014). 2.
[57] Greydanus, Huff & Omar (2012). 387.

let her continue when she falls pregnant. Instead, Callie is asked to leave high school and enroll in a special school for teen mothers with a parenting-based curriculum. Her focus is shoved away from her talents and passions and towards being a mother. The general feeling evoked by the film is one of wasted talent, the wistful wondering what might have been if only Callie hadn't become pregnant.

2001's Riding in Cars with Boys is based on the true story of Beverly Donofrio, a 15-year-old girl whose unexpected pregnancy shatters her dreams of becoming a professional writer. The film examines the impact of choices, and the theme that one bad decision can ruin your whole life. Beverly goes from a promising student to a 15-year-old wife and mother, living in a run-down house and desperately trying to scrape together enough time to study for her High School Equivalency Certificate. As the story continues, Beverly becomes more defeated as she recognizes that the life she had dreamed of is out of reach. She feels trapped by her circumstances. Eventually, Beverly does manage to publish her own book, a memoir of her personal struggles. Despite achieving her goal, there is a sadness about her; a constant bitterness that she could have done more with her life had she not lost so many years to motherhood. She tells her son, Jason, that she feels responsible for her mistakes, but that she doesn't blame him for any of them. Beverly's story is a cautionary tale that a mistake can cost you dearly, but that it may still be possible to claw your way back to where you want to be.

Conversely, there are a handful of films that feature young mothers thriving and achieving their dreams. Where the Heart Is (2000) tells the story of a 17 year old girl, Novalie Nation, who is left barefoot and alone when her boyfriend abandons her during a cross-country drive. After giving birth in a Walmart, Novalie gains the support of her community and makes a number of close friends. She eventually overcomes the difficulties of being a new mother and achieves her dream of becoming a professional photographer. Where the Heart is paints a hopeful story of teenage motherhood. It counters the bleak idea that teenage pregnancy marks the end of a young woman's life, and instead shows that resourcefulness and resilience can help a teenage mother to achieve her goals while raising a child.

On the flip side, we see a host of ambitious young girls who do not become pregnant during their movies, but who find pregnancy to be a looming threat. Many of these characters choose to abstain from sex so that they won't have to give up their dreams, or grapple with their choice to have sex because of the potential ruin it could bring.

When this storyline presents itself, it often features a protagonist who is themselves the result of a teen pregnancy. They have seen firsthand the sacrifices that their mothers had to make in order to raise them, and may feel a sense of guilt or regret that they didn't get to live the lives that they dreamed of. These characters are often shown to feel a strong desire to make their mothers proud, and to do more with their lives than their mothers did. For them, teen pregnancy feels like a very real danger, and something that they desperately want to avoid. Interestingly, real-life statistics show that children of teen parents are more likely to become pregnant as teenagers when compared to children whose parents had reached adulthood at the time of their birth.[58] It seems that for children of teen parents, the threat of teen pregnancy feels more real, and in actual fact may be a greater risk for them.

Two of the films I examined explore this particular trope. The protagonist of Drop Dead Gorgeous (1999), Amber Atkins, throws all her efforts into winning a local beauty pageant as a ticket out of her small-town life. The daughter of a teen-mother and former beauty queen, Amber sees winning the pageant as the first step towards achieving her dreams, and a way to move beyond the trailer-park life she is currently living. Amber isn't particularly interested in dating or sex, and her efforts are mostly focused on winning and achieving her dreams.

Just one year later, Looking for Alibrandi (2000) dove deeper into this trope. Josie Alibrandi is 17, the same

---

[58] Poynter (2014). 3.

age her mother was when she gave birth to her. Josie's sights are firmly focused on finishing high school at the top of her class so that she can study law at university. She has made up her mind that she will be the first woman in her family to have a say in how her life turns out. Josie's birth was a source of enormous upheaval for her mother, who became estranged from her parents and had to give up her dream of becoming a writer to raise her daughter. Although Josie's family is close and comfortable, she still feels a prickle of fear when she considers the possibility of her life being derailed the way her mother's was. During the course of the film, Josie begins her first serious relationship, and starts to consider losing her virginity. Although there are a host of factors she weighs up when deciding if she should have sex for the first time, the fear of becoming pregnant and losing control over her life is definitely a strong consideration for Josie.

Another movie that explores the disruptive power of an unplanned pregnancy is Down to You (2000). In this film, college student Imogen has a pregnancy scare. While waiting for the results of a pregnancy test, Imogen imagines what her life would be like if she had a baby. She becomes overwhelmed by the possibility that she would have to give up her studies and her dream career in order to care for a baby that she doesn't want. When she discovers that she is not actually pregnant, she is relieved. However, the scare drives a wedge between her and her partner Al, and she begins to distance herself from him sexually. The fear of ruining her life by falling pregnant is great enough to cause Imogen to withdraw from the loving relationship she had enjoyed with Al, and become more focused on her studies.

Interestingly, whenever a film uses teen pregnancy as a warning, that warning is always squarely directed at young girls. I couldn't find any examples of movies that act as a cautionary tale to boys, discouraging them from having sex in case they get their partner pregnant and ruin their lives. This may have a lot to do with the fact that the impact of teen pregnancy is much greater on young women than it is on their partners. While boys are often able to walk away from the situation if they don't want to be a part of it, the young women who become pregnant have no choice but to deal with the repercussions. Teenage boys who father children are much less likely to have their futures impacted, and they are able to continue with their education and careers without taking responsibility if they so choose. In Juno (2007), the title character points out how unfair it is that the father of her baby doesn't have to deal with the responsibility of being pregnant, that his life gets to carry on as normal while she has to deal with the stigma and physical toll of carrying their baby. This astute observation points out the stark differences in how unplanned pregnancy impacts the lives of teen girls and their male partners.

The Profile of a Teen Mother.

There have been a number of studies conducted to try to identify risk factors that may predict teen pregnancy. These studies have attempted to generate an understanding of the type of person that is more likely to be impacted by teen pregnancy, to inform interventions to lower the rates of teen pregnancy. The results of these studies have built a loose profile of the typical teen parent, and I wanted to take a look at how depictions of teen pregnancy in films matches the statistics.

There is evidence to suggest that one of the strongest factors that may predict the likelihood of a teenager falling pregnant is whether there has been another instance of teen pregnancy in their family. Teenagers with a family history of teen pregnancy are twice as likely to fall pregnant themselves when compared with peers who do not have a family history of teen pregnancy.[59] This is true for children of teen parents, but also includes siblings of teen parents.

Another factor which may indicate that a teenager is at greater risk of teen pregnancy is low economic status and living in a poorer neighborhood.[60] This is true for both young women and young men. A troubled childhood or history of abuse also puts a teenager at greater risk of unplanned pregnancy than peers who have had a more stable upbringing.[61] Also,

---

[59] Poynter (2014). 14.
[60] Poynter (2014). 3.
[61] Greydanus, Huff & Omar (2012). 394.

of the teenagers who have one unplanned pregnancy, 35% will go on to become pregnant a second time before they turn 20.[62]

Of the films I watched for my research, several of them feature teen parents that fit this profile. The film protagonist who most clearly matches the picture of the typical teen parent is Novalie Nation from Where the Heart Is. Novalie is herself the daughter of a teen mother. She is depicted as being not particularly well educated and has very little money. Novalie's best friend, Lexie has four children and gave birth to the first when she was only 15. Lexie talks about how she kept searching for a father for her children, but each man she thought would be a suitable daddy left her alone and pregnant. Both women in this movie are shown as hopeful and fulfilled despite the challenges of motherhood.

In Save the Last Dance (2001), we see a young mother raising her son with the support of her family. Chenille continues to attend high school while her mother

---

[62] Greydanus, Huff & Omar (2012). 394.

assists with childcare for her baby son, Christopher. Chenille lives in a poor neighborhood in South Side Chicago where there is a lot of criminal activity. Her former partner isn't particularly involved in her son's upbringing, despite her efforts to include him. Chenille is shown to be a caring mother who is working with the support of her family to provide for her son and complete her education.

While Save the Last Dance shows a young mother working to rise up from a position of poverty, Riding in Cars with Boys depicts a promising young woman being dragged down by a partner from a lower economic background. In this film, Beverly's boyfriend, Ray, is from a much poorer family than she is. Ray has not known many of the privileges that Beverly has grown up with, and his childhood was troubled. Ray's employment prospects are very limited, and he ultimately begins taking drugs and dabbling in illegal activity. After a series of disappointments, Beverly forces Ray to leave, believing that their son's life would be better without his influence. Interestingly, Beverly's life does not immediately improve once Ray is out of the picture. She spends a good chunk of the film working multiple jobs, living in poverty and even tries selling drugs in an attempt to make more money for her son. It takes years of hard work for her to pull herself out of the hole she's in, highlighting that Ray isn't solely to blame for the rough turn Beverly's life has taken.

Another interesting statistic that is worth looking at is the finding that approximately half of all teen pregnancies occur within 6 months of the teenager becoming sexually active.[63] Around 65% of teenage pregnancies occur with the mother's first partner.[64] The majority of the films I examined follow this trend, depicting teens falling pregnant very soon after they begin having sex. In Saved (2004), Mary becomes pregnant the very first time she has sex. Riding in Cars With Boy's Beverly and her best friend Faye both fall pregnant soon after they begin experimenting with sex. These depictions not only reflect the findings of the statistics, but caution teens that it can be very easy

---

[63] Greydanus, Huff & Omar (2012). 389.
[64] Carvalho Sant'Anna et al (2006).

to fall pregnant, and that you can become pregnant even the very first time you have sex.

The average age of teen mothers in film depictions also matches the statistics. On average, most teenage mothers are approximately 16 years of age.[65] Most of the teen mothers we see in the films I have discussed hover around this age, with some a little older (Novalie from Where the Heart Is) and some a little younger (Beverly Donofrio from Riding in Cars with Boys). Generally speaking, the media depictions of teen pregnancy seem to mirror the statistics fairly closely.

One discrepancy that I found between the media representation of teen pregnancy and the statistics on the subject was the prevalence of complications in teen pregnancies. In the movies, most teen pregnancies are shown as being relatively uneventful, progressing along a fairly predictable path and ending with a textbook delivery. In reality, young mothers may experience physical complications during pregnancy and birth. This is particularly true if they

---

[65] Carvalho Sant'Anna (2006).

are at the younger end of the spectrum and have not finished puberty when they fall pregnant. Nutritional problems are significant, as the young mother may still be growing herself, and her diet may not meet the needs of her own growing body as well as that of her child. Additionally, younger mothers who are not fully developed may experience complications during birth.[66] The only film that I watched which touches on this subject is The Opposite of Sex. Deedee experiences a hemorrhage during her labour which quickly becomes serious. So serious, in fact, that Deedee almost dies as a result. As most of the movies that feature teen pregnancy are either comedic, or only mention the pregnancy as part of a sub-plot, it makes sense that these more serious complications aren't discussed at length.

Contraception and teen pregnancy

Although I've already discussed contraceptives in the previous chapter of this book, I did want to look at the discussion of contraception as it relates to teen pregnancy. In the majority of films from the 1990's

---

[66] Carvalho Sant'Anna et al (2006).

and 2000's where a teen pregnancy occurs, contraceptives are not used at all. In Where The Heart is, there is no explicit discussion of whether Novalie was using contraception at the time she fell pregnant with her first child. However, she does have a sexual encounter later in the film where she doesn't use any form of birth control. She rejoices when she gets her period, and it is heavily implied that no birth control was employed when she became pregnant with her daughter. Her friend Lexie tells her that she's always used the "poke and pray" method, which is clearly not very effective as Lexie has four children, all unplanned. Interestingly, research suggests that adolescent mums are more likely to use contraceptives, and use them correctly, after they have had one child. However, this finding was applicable to teen mothers who were supported by a multi-disciplinary care team during their pregnancies and after birth.[67] It may be the case that women who do not have access to comprehensive medical advice and support, such as the characters in this film, may continue to rely on the birth control

[67] Sant'Anna et al (2007).

methods that are familiar to them, even if they have not worked in the past.

In Saved, Looking for Alibrandi and Riding in Cars with Boys, no contraceptives are used by any of the protagonists who fall pregnant. Real world studies have shown that in the USA, the majority of teen pregnancies happen to teens who are not using birth control.[68]

I could find only one depiction of failed birth control that resulted in a teen pregnancy. In The Opposite of Sex (1998), sixteen-year-old Deedee falls pregnant after she and her partner use the "pull out method" and he fails to pull out in time. The "Pull Out Method" refers to with Withdrawal Method, where the penis is removed from the vagina before ejaculation to prevent pregnancy. According to Planned Parenthood, the Withdrawal Method is one of the least effective forms of birth control, with about 1 in 5 couples who rely on this method falling pregnant every year.[69] The

---

[68] Greydanus, Huff & Omar (2012). 389.
[69] Planned Parenthood Federation of America (2020).

Withdrawal Method may fail for a variety of reasons, including the presence of sperm in pre-cum which is present well before ejaculation, and the inability of the male partner to correctly time withdrawal. It is particularly difficult for teenagers to execute this method, as it requires a strong understanding of one's own sexual response, and teens may lack the experience to be able to know precisely when to pull out. The Withdrawal Method may be attractive to teenagers because it doesn't cost anything and seems fairly easy to execute. The Opposite of Sex's Deedee is depicted as very confident in her own sexuality and sexual knowledge, but clearly she has overestimated her ability to avoid a pregnancy using this unreliable method of birth control.

What to do with the baby?

Interestingly, there isn't a lot of variation in the outcomes of the teen pregnancies which were depicted in the films I watched for my research. In practically every instance, the teen mother ends up keeping her child. In most instances, there isn't even a discussion about what she will do, most of these characters instantly decide that they will keep their baby. Occasionally, adoption will be briefly entertained as an idea, but is often quickly dismissed. The only instance I could find where adoption is actually carried out is The Opposite of Sex. After a brief attempt at motherhood, Deedee concludes that she is not cut out to care for a child, and that her son would be better off living with her brother. It takes a long time for this decision to be reached, and it is clear throughout the film that Deedee really isn't interested in becoming a mother.

One topic that is mostly absent from teen movies of this period is the subject of abortion. Although there is rarely much debate about what a teen mother should do with her baby, it is even rarer that she would consider terminating her pregnancy in films from this era. Abortion is seldom mentioned as a possibility, unlike films from the later 2000's which often do posit abortion as a potential route for young women who find themselves pregnant. This is interesting, as up to 40% of all teen pregnancies are terminated.[70] It is

[70] Greydanus, Huff and Omar (2012). 387.

estimated that around 10% of mothers who give birth as teenagers attempted to abort the pregnancy themselves. Surveys of teen mothers have revealed that more of them would have aborted their pregnancies but cost and access to health care present significant barriers.[71]   The only film I watched which shows a young woman seriously considering ending her pregnancy is Riding in Cars with Boys. In this film Beverly strongly toys with the idea of attempting to induce a miscarriage after her friend tells her that her aunt lost a baby after falling down the stairs. Beverly tries to throw herself down the stairs but is unable to actually go through with it.   There are no discussions about the possibility of visiting a doctor for a medical termination, which may partially be attributed to the fact that this film is set in the 1960's and abortion was even more taboo during this time period.

Attitudes towards teen mothers

One of the important aspects of teen pregnancy that is touched on in many teen films is the social impact and stigma that surrounds teen mothers.   Social

---

[71] Carvahlho Sant'Anna et al. (2006).

standing and popularity is important to teenagers, and many young people can think of nothing worse than losing their friends or being excluded by their peers. Social attitudes towards young girls who become pregnant are rarely favourable, and this can cause a huge amount of distress for young women who are already in an extremely vulnerable position.

Religious attitudes towards premarital sex and unplanned pregnancy can often create a hostile environment for young mothers. This is particularly upsetting for young women who have strong faith, for whom the church has previously been a source of support and comfort. To be suddenly cast out by your support network is jarring. Coupled with the idea that their pregnancy is a punishment for sinful behaviour, this creates a dangerous environment for a young mother, and may have a terrible impact on her mental health.

One of the most notable discussions of this topic is contained in 2004's Saved. This film is set is a very strict Christian community, where Christian values and behaviour are heralded as the gold standard. People who do not adhere to a Christian faith and values are treated as outsiders. When the protagonist, Mary, becomes pregnant she hides her pregnancy from almost everyone in her life. She knows that if her school or family found out that she was pregnant, she would be cast out and treated like a criminal. Mary already feels alone and scared, and she cannot face the possibility of losing her friends and family. As a result, she conceals her pregnancy well into her third trimester, when it is no longer possible to hide. Religious opposition to teen pregnancy is also depicted in Where the Heart Is, as Novalie faces discrimination and hate mail from religious groups, who even go so far to kidnap her child because they believe that Novalie is an unsuitable parent.

Teen mothers may also face unwanted sexual attention from their male peers. In Crossroads (2002), Mimi has to fend off advances from boys who believe that she will be willing to have sex with them based on the simple fact that she is pregnant. They make the assumption that, because Mimi has obviously had sex, she is promiscuous and eager to sleep with anyone. This unfortunate depiction of the pregnant girl as a "ruined woman" stems from the elevated value of virginity and the aforementioned idea that a girl who is pregnant has destroyed her life. In Mimi's case, she has become pregnant as a result of sexual assault, not through consensual sexual intercourse. When the viewer learns this, it becomes easy to understand why Mimi doesn't want to have sex with anyone else. It's important to note that just because a girl has had consensual sex on one occasion doesn't mean that she is willing do it again. The mere fact that a girl is pregnant isn't necessarily evidence of sexual promiscuity or willingness to engage in further sexual contact.

Mimi finds support from her friends, who listen to her and assist her through this difficult time in her life. In many of the films which depict teen pregnancies, the protagonist may be shunned by their wider community or families, but often finds comfort in one or two trusted friends. In Saved, Mary makes friends with two other teens who are treated as social outcasts, one because he's in a wheelchair and another because she's Jewish. The three of them form a supportive posse, and help Mary throughout her pregnancy. In Riding in Cars With Boys, Beverly's best friend Faye falls pregnant at the same time she does. The two of them cling to each other through the shared experience of pregnancy and parenthood. They can relate to one another's struggles and develop an "us against the world" attitude as they see their other friends graduating and moving away to college.

Teen movies often use pregnancy as a cautionary tale, warning young girls about the dangers of teen pregnancy. There's a strong undercurrent of fear in these tales which highlight the moral, financial and social pitfalls that can abound as a result of unprotected sex. On the flipside, many of these stories temper the message with depictions of support from friendship groups and hardworking mothers who manage to overcome the challenges of parenthood to ultimately achieve their dreams. The overarching message seems to be that it's best to avoid getting pregnant as a teenager, because it's a difficult

145

situation to be in, but that if it does happen to you, the picture isn't completely hopeless.

Chapter 8
LGBTQI Representation

"It's easy to be a prude when you aren't attracted to him", But I'm a Cheerleader.

One topic that I especially wanted to examine when researching this book is the representation of LGBTQI+ young people in teen movies. As a teenager, I spent a lot of time questioning my own sexuality. I was attracted to boys and had many relationships during my teen years, but I also experienced crushes on girls. I was powerfully drawn to depictions of lesbians in film and television, although they were fairly minimal and often the representations weren't complimentary. Something about those stories spoke to me, and it would be years before I connected the dots and realised I was bisexual. Queer cinema is a particular interest of mine, and a number of fantastic queer films were released during this time period. In addition to the films that told LGBTQI stories, I also wanted to look at the ways in which those characters and stories were woven into more mainstream media of the time.

The late 90's and early 2000's were a period of seismic change for the LGBTQI community. Attitudes were slowly beginning to shift, and it was gradually becoming more acceptable to be publicly homosexual. It was becoming more common for celebrities to be open about their sexuality. I vividly remember watching a news report on Ellen Degeneres's public coming out and feeling deep in my bones that this was a Big Moment. Slowly, the stigma around homosexuality was being worn away, and it was becoming Ok to be gay. On the other hand, the fear and disgust for the queer community that was generated by the AIDS crisis of the late 80's and early 90's was still lingering, and many used AIDS as an excuse to be openly hostile and fearful of gay people. This was a time when attitudes were shifting gradually towards more public acceptance of queerness, but violence, anger and homophobia were still very much alive. This changing attitude is apparent in the films I looked at. While there are several positive depictions of queer sexuality, more often than not gay characters are treated with ridicule, confusion and erasure. They're rarely the main character, usually a sidekick and frequently they're the butt of the joke.

Homophobia and slurs

One thing that I found incredibly jarring while watching these films was the frequent use of homophobic slurs. They popped up with alarming regularity, and were commonly used to shame and belittle. Slurs such as "Homo", "Faggot" and "Bender" were used over and over. It was quite shocking to me, because in the two decades since these films were made, these words have slipped out of the acceptable vocabulary of the average person. Now considered to be deeply offensive, these slurs are tossed about quite casually in a lot of the films that I watched as part of my research. In many instances, they are often used to bully and belittle an unpopular character, or someone who is considered "different". In Bring it On, the male cheerleaders are regularly called "fags" by the football team. When a rebellious new girl tries out for the cheerleading squad, one of the cheerleaders puts her down by calling her "A big dykey loser". In Jawbreaker the popular girls refer to a group of unpopular girls as "carpet munchers". Homosexuality is seen as something to be ashamed of, and calling someone gay or a lesbian is the ultimate insult.

An extension on the prevalence of homophobic slurs is the negative attitude towards homosexuals. Naturally, if you are calling someone "gay" as a means of insulting them, then you must also feel that being gay is something shameful, disgusting and negative. The use of slurs is just one way of displaying homophobic attitudes. Another way that homophobia plays out in the media is through the repeated depiction of young people (particularly young men) being upset or offended if they are mistaken for being gay. Naturally, if you believe that homosexuality is something terrible, then you wouldn't want someone to think that you are gay. In Can't Hardly Wait, Mike is horrified when someone at his graduation party loudly calls him a "fag" in front of the other guests. What is particularly telling about this scene is the fact that over the course of the story, Mike has been abandoned by his friends, rejected by his former girlfriend and has had his idyllic fantasy of college life shattered by his hero. And yet, it is being publicly labelled a "fag" that triggers Mike to break down in tears when he pours out his story to a confidante. To Mike, having a room full of people think he might be gay is infinitely worse than any of the other upsetting things that have occurred that day. In other films, such as The New Guy and American Pie 2, we see other male characters going to great lengths to prove that they aren't gay, or worring that the way they speak or present themselves will give people the impression of homosexuality.

On the flipside, there are also a number of depictions of characters who are actually homosexual, but are either attempting to keep their sexuality hidden or have not yet come to terms with their sexuality. In Cruel Intentions, the character Greg actively seeks out men to sleep with, but as soon as they've finished having sex, he behaves as though he's disgusted with them and tells them to leave. Later in the film, one of the lead characters blackmails Greg, threatening to tell his friends that he's gay unless he follows their orders.

Greg is mortified that the people around him will reject him if they find out that he's a homosexual. Another example of this trope is the character Banky Edwards in Chasing Amy. Banky is openly homophobic, using frequent homophobic slurs, questioning the validity of lesbianism and generally behaving in a bigoted manner towards anything he perceives to be "gay". As the film progresses, it becomes clear that Banky is actually gay, but has not yet managed to admit this to himself. It's unclear whether Banky is struggling with his sexuality because of his internalised homophobia, or whether the homophobic behaviour is a façade that he's adopted to "prove" to himself that he can't be gay. Either way, it's not uncommon to see a character who is inwardly struggling with their sexuality, but outwardly rejecting homosexuality.

There are also examples of homophobia directed at female characters. In Mean Girls, the popular girl group "The Plastics" ruin a less popular girls' reputation by spreading a rumour that she's a lesbian. The Faculty tips this storyline on it's head by having the character Stokely spread a rumour that she's a lesbian, in an effort to keep people away from her because she prefers to be alone. In each instance, we see the idea that lesbianism is undesirable, and any girl who displays same-sex-attraction should be kept at arm's length. We rarely, if ever, see a queer character who is a part of the popular group, and if they are, then they're usually closeted or only on the fringes of the it-group.

The Sapphic Spectacle

There's a strange push-and-pull of reactions when it comes to the depictions of lesbians in film. As I've already mentioned, same-sex attraction, or even the suggestion of the same, may be the reason why a young girl is ostracized or bullied. On the other hand, lesbian interactions are often shown as a spectacle, something beautiful and entertaining to watch. Public displays of affection between women may be seen as exciting, subversive and erotic. In Mean Girls, the very same girls who tease Janis for supposedly being a lesbian make out with one another at a party while the boys watch them. For them, it's not OK to actually be gay, but to perform homosexual acts to impress members of the opposite sex is perfectly acceptable. In American Pie 2, a group of young men assume that two women who live together are lesbians. When they confront them, the women kiss and touch one another's breasts and buttocks to arouse and entice the boys. The women aren't gay, but they enjoy putting on a performance to titillate and tease the men who are watching. In Chasing Amy, Banky and Holden are captivated when they watch two lesbians kiss, and Banky makes a number of inappropriate comments to encourage the women to take their kissing further and to allow him to watch. Unlike the previous two examples, the women who are partaking are actually gay, and they make it very clear that their affections aren't intended as a performance for the male gaze.

This type of attitude towards lesbian interactions isn't terribly surprising. Girl-on-girl scenes are one of the most popular types of pornography for young men.[72] It seems that this type of material is aimed at perpetuating a male fantasy of watching two beautiful women enjoying one another's bodies, with the

[72] Australian Men's Health Magazine (September 2019)

possibility that the viewer could imagine themselves joining in. The male attitude towards the women's attraction could be that the women are heterosexual but are putting on a show for his benefit, happy to turn their attentions to him. Alternatively, it could be that they don't necessarily believe that lesbianism really exists. In Chasing Amy, Banky tells his friend Holden that he doesn't actually believe that there is such a thing as a real lesbian, and that every woman needs a "deep dicking" once in a while. Banky concedes that while there are women who are attracted to one another, the presence of a willing male partner would override those feelings and they would be unable to resist. In his mind, the attraction to a man is superior to same-sex attraction and would supersede any suggestions of lesbianism. This idea that lesbianism isn't real, or that it's just for women who haven't found the right guy is deeply homophobic.

Interestingly, the core premise of Chasing Amy is a lesbian questioning her sexuality when she falls in love with a man. In this film, Alyssa is very comfortable with her sexuality. Although she has slept with men in the past, she has accepted that she is a lesbian because "women feel right" to her. When she falls in love with Holden, this turns her entire view of herself on its head. She becomes deeply confused about what this attraction means and spends most of the movie grappling with her sexuality. Although this film has been criticized for supposedly illustrating that even the most confident lesbian can have her head turned by the right man, I take a different view of the message of Chasing Amy. Rather than seeing Alyssa as a lesbian who "turns straight" when she falls in love with a man, I think that Chasing Amy is a film about a woman whose sexuality evolves beyond the label she had originally placed upon herself. For many people, the way they describe their sexuality in their teens or early twenties may not remain static for the remainder of their lives. As we grow and meet new people and have new experiences, we uncover new parts of ourselves. For some, we may find that the one label fits for our whole lives. For others, our experiences cause us to question and expand the definitions that have previously applied. In the case of Alyssa, I think we see a woman who previously identified as a lesbian, but who has now come to explore the possibility that perhaps she's bisexual or pansexual. Her lesbian identity isn't erased when she falls in love with Holden, but her understanding of her sexuality expands to include another possibility.

How do gay people have sex anyway?

For a lot of heterosexual folks, the topic of gay sex is one that raises some eyebrows as well as a host of questions. The majority of sex education talks only about penis-in-vagina sex. Any other sexual acts, if discussed, are presented as foreplay or a prelude to "real sex". So, a lot of people feel baffled how homosexual couples make love if P-in-V sex is off the table. Some would even question whether the intimacy they share even counts as sex. In Chasing Amy, Holden and Alyssa share a conversation that discusses this very topic. Holden tells Alyssa that his definition of sex only includes vaginal penetration, so oral sex doesn't count as sex to him. Alyssa mentions that she doesn't use a strap-on to penetrate a partner and he seems genuinely confused about how she can be having sex if there isn't a phallus involved. Alyssa's sexual encounters most frequently involve oral sex, fingering and occasionally fisting. Holden is still skeptical that any of those acts actually count as "real sex".

The British film A Beautiful Thing tells the story of two young boys who fall in love and are exploring their sexuality. As their relationship progresses, they experiment with a variety of ways to be intimate, including massage and passionate kissing. At one point, they read a magazine article together about "frottage", which refers to grinding the penis against a partner while fully or partially clothed. The article they read presents frottage as a way to avoid HIV because there is no penetration. I find A Beautiful Thing interesting because it turns away from the idea that for homosexual men, their sexual expression is confined to anal sex. In this film the characters are beginning to explore their sensuality together, and we see them enjoying intimacy in a variety of ways.

Another film which gives us a beautiful example of sexual exploration in a same-sex couple is But I'm a

Cheerleader. In this film, the protagonist Megan and her love interest Graham (who is also a woman) share a tender sex scene that involves kissing, caressing, massage, sucking on fingers, stroking thighs and running fingers through hair. It is scenes like this that show the variety of intimate acts that can be enjoyed by all couples, not only those in same-sex partnerships. Although we don't see any penetrative acts and no genitals are involved, it's clear that the interaction between these characters is erotic and sensual.

In Boys Don't Cry, there are several sex scenes between a transgender man, Brandon, and his girlfriend Lana. Early in the film, Lana doesn't realise that Brandon is transgender even after they've had sex. The sex scenes aren't entirely specific about what Lana and Brandon are doing, but from what we do see there is some digital penetration and the suggestion that Brandon uses a "packer" dildo to penetrate Lana. Although we see a lot of erotic kissing and touching, the actual mechanics of the sex that they have is shrouded in mystery. This echoes the questions that many cisgender and straight people have about queer sex, and offers few answers about how the sex happens. It's clear from their interactions that Lana and Brandon are both satisfied with their physical relationship, and Brandon mentions earlier in the film that he's very successful with women and is often "the best boyfriend they've ever had". Even if we don't see exactly what they're doing, there can be little doubt that their sexual explorations are exciting, fun and fulfilling for both parties.

It is important to note that sex education programs during the 90s and 2000's rarely included discussion of sex between same-sex couples. Such programs tended to focus heavily on penis-in-vagina sex, often excluding discussion of any other sexual acts. Even now, sex education tends to be very heteronormative, centering heterosexual sex and largely ignoring any sexual interaction that lies outside this scope. For this reason, people who find themselves attracted to people of the same sex often have to do their own research and exploration into what sex can look like for homosexual couples. As I mentioned earlier, the film A Beautiful Thing features two young gay men looking through books and gay magazines for answers to their questions about physical intimacy. Once again, we see how a dearth of information about sexuality leads to teenagers having to do their own research, which can be challenging if there is a lack of reputable information to provide answers.

Sex can be so much more than just penis-in-vagina, and expanding the definition of sex opens up a whole world of understanding and exploration. It's so important to look at the different things that can fall under the umbrella of "sex" because it makes the definition much more inclusive. It begins to encompass all kinds of expression and doesn't limit sex to just one single act. In recent years, these discussions have become more widespread, but it's exciting to see those ideas and questions beginning to germinate and spring forward in these handful of movies from the early 2000's.

The Predatory Queer

Another facet of the homophobic representations is the idea of homosexuals as predators. There's a long-standing stereotype of the predatory homosexual.

This trope shows up in a number of different ways, and paints homosexual people as sexually aggressive and untrustworthy. It's a very damaging stereotype, because it's pervasiveness in pop culture leads people to internalise the idea that people who are queer can't be trusted, will take advantage of people and won't respect sexual boundaries. One of the most notable representations of this trope in the films I studied was in The Opposite of Sex. The protagonist, Deedee, is disgusted by the idea of homosexuality and repeatedly voices her homophobia. Her brother, Bill, is a teacher and she questions whether it's safe for a gay man to hold that position. Towards the end of the film, she states that she's uncomfortable with Bill changing her son's nappy and looking at his genitals. She has a deeply-held idea that gay men are predators and that they can't be trusted, especially around young men or children. In Eurotrip, there's a scene where a stereotypically effeminate man makes a number of unwelcome physical advances on a group of teenagers on a train. Each time the train goes through a tunnel and the carriage is plunged into darkness, the man makes a move and the teenagers are shown looking more and more distressed each time it happens. This trope effectively treats gay men in particular as dangerous, and sets them apart as something to be feared rather than accepted.

Pray the Gay Away

Queer sexuality is sometimes thought of as a deviation from the norm. If heterosexuality is the 'straight" path, the right and normal way to progress through life, then being gay is seen to be a detour off the right track. Heteronormativity is the idea that heterosexuality is the default setting for all humans, the baseline or what's "normal". When we view sexuality this way, then any other form of sexual expression may be seen as abnormal, or less desirable than the default. It may also create the idea that being gay is a choice, and that a person could then get over their homosexual impulses and live a heterosexual lifestyle.

This assumption is the basis for conversion therapy, a harmful practice in which a person who is expressing non-heterosexual desires undergoes therapy and exercises to "deprogram" them. This therapy may take on a variety of forms, many of which are physically harmful and ethically problematic. They are particularly prominent in religious communities who believe that homosexuality is sinful. The idea that sexuality is a choice, that one can simply rewire themselves to change who they are attracted to has been used in a number of films that feature conversion storylines.

In Saved, Mary is horrified when her boyfriend tells her that he's gay. They are both deeply religious, and Mary is fearful for his soul. She takes it upon herself to help him. She loses her virginity to him in the hope that this will "fix" him. Mary believes that it is God's will that she assists her boyfriend and that if she makes this sacrifice, then Dean's heterosexuality will be restored. Soon after, Dean's parents ship him off for conversion therapy when they find homosexual pornography in his bedroom. Ultimately, we see that the therapy hasn't worked at all, as Dean brings a boyfriend home with him when he returns.

On the other side of the coin, But I'm A Cheerleader shows the attempted conversion of a young woman, Megan. Megan's parents are religious, and they are fearful that if their daughter continues to pursue her same-sex impulses that she will have a difficult and unhappy life. But I'm a Cheerleader is a very clever parody of conversion therapies, which plays on stereotypical tropes of homosexuality and gender roles to show just how ridiculous this type of thinking is. Once again, the conversion therapy only serves to cement Megan's identity as a lesbian, and she leaves the facility with a woman that she's fallen in love with.

Bisexual erasure

There is very little discussion of bisexuality in the teen films of the 90's and 2000's. This may be a reflection of the skepticism that surrounds bisexual identities. Even now, there is a significant amount of bisexual erasure, with many people claiming that bisexuality is a myth or a phase. There's a lingering idea that bisexuality is a transitory period, and that people who claim to be bisexual will one day choose to either be straight or identify as gay. Once again, this idea perpetuates the myth that sexuality is a choice, rather than something that's ingrained. Bisexuality is rarely discussed in these films, and when it is, it's usually in a manner that's dismissive.

In The Opposite of Sex, Deedee sleeps with her brother's boyfriend as a way of "testing" if he's really gay. Deedee tells him that he can't possibly know if he's gay if he's never tried sleeping with a woman. After they have sex, Matt tells his friends that he's bisexual, because he enjoyed sleeping with Deedee. At the end of the film Deedee concludes the story by saying that Matt has reached "the final stage of bisexuality" where he has admitted to himself that he's gay. This illustrates that attitude that bisexual people are just easing themselves into admitting that they're homosexual. In Chasing Amy, when Amy tells her lesbian friends that she's fallen in love with a man, most of them are horrified. They aren't supportive of her and treat her questioning of her sexuality as a betrayal. This scene rings really true to me, as a bisexual woman. Sometimes I have felt unwelcome in queer spaces, particularly when I'm dating a cisgender man. I've often felt "not queer enough" to attend Pride events and have faced open derision from lesbian friends when I've met a new male partner. This scene paints a really telling picture of the ways in which bisexuals may not feel at home in queer spaces, while simultaneously feeling unwelcome in the vanilla, straight world.

For me personally, I feel that the lack of positive representations of bisexual characters in films from the 90's and 2000's made it more challenging for me to identify my own bisexuality. When I first started experiencing attraction to women, I became deeply confused and frightened of these feelings. I knew that I was attracted to boys, because I'd had a number of crushes on boys and even a few boyfriends. I had kissed boys and enjoyed the experience. But when I began having crushes on girls, I began to wonder if it meant that I was secretly gay. I spent years grappling with this question, trying to figure out what my feelings meant. I remember thinking about the characters in films who briefly identified as bisexual, only to later come out as gay. I truly believe that if there had been at least a few positive depictions of bisexual characters in the media that I was consuming, that it would have shortened the time it took for me to come to terms with my own bisexuality. Had there been a representation in film that mirrored my own feelings, I would have had something to relate to. As I've said many times, I recognize that the role of film is to entertain rather than educate, but I also feel that the dearth of bisexual characters in mainstream media at this time definitely made it more challenging for me to identify and then accept my own bisexuality.

Figuring out and coming out

Adolescence is typically the time when our sexuality begins to present itself, and it's usually at this stage of life that a person begins to get an inkling that they might not be straight. There are three stages of a person realising their homosexual identity.[73] The first stage is feeling "different" from their peers. This may be recognizing that their friends are starting to develop an interest in the opposite sex that they aren't feeling, or noticing that they don't' seem to enjoy flirting or physical intimacy as much as their friends.

---

[73] Greydan us and Omar (2014).

In But I'm a Cheerleader, Megan is talking to her friend about kissing her boyfriend and asks "don't you just hate it when they do that?". She feels detached and uninterested when her boyfriend kisses her. When her friend says she loves being kissed, Megan wonders if perhaps her boyfriend is doing it wrong. In A Beautiful Thing, Jamie and Ste bond over the fact that they don't fancy girls in magazines, and neither of them is interested in any of the girls they go to school with.

The second stage is having a crush on a person of the same gender. It may take some time for the person to realise that they're experiencing a crush, and may have some conflict as to whether they like the person, or simply admire them and want to be like them. In Boogie Nights, we see this type of relationship play out when Scottie develops a crush on Dirk. Scottie begins dressing like Dirk and emulating him in other ways, such as buying the same car. It seems to take some time for Scottie to realise that he actually has a crush on Dirk. When he finally tells Dirk how he feels, he is brutally disappointed that Dirk doesn't feel the same way about him.

The third stage is becoming aware of homosexual orientation. This stage might be followed by a "coming out" phase, where the person tells their friends and family about their sexual orientation. There may never be an official "coming out", but the person may simply continue living their life in a way that feels right to them. In Clueless, the character of Christian is revealed to be gay, even though he never actually comes out to his friends. We see him flirting with a bartender and dancing with a boy at a party. His friends seem to accept him without him ever explicitly telling them that he's gay. In Dead Man on Campus, two characters fabricate a story about being gay to cover up a secret. When they tell their friends that they're gay, they are met with full support and genuine care. Even though the characters aren't actually gay, it's quite sweet that all their mates would still be there for them if they were.

Depictions of the realisation of one's sexuality might be an important turning point for viewers. For young people in the nineties and 2000's who were beginning to question their own identity, seeing a character go through something similar would be reassuring and affirming. It might make them feel less alone, particularly during a time when homosexuality was only just beginning to be widely accepted and there was still a great deal of negative attitudes towards people who identified as queer.

I feel as though the films from the 90's and 2000's are a snapshot of a changing time for the LGBTQI community. The overall attitude towards characters who identify as homosexual is negative, and there are plenty of examples of violence and harassment of gay characters. The prevalence of homosexual slurs and the disgust exhibited towards homosexuality is evidence of a general wariness and lack of acceptance of gay people. Among these scenes though are glimmers of hope, a few scenes that show queer people living happy lives, enjoying moments of romance and genuine intimacy with a partner of the same gender. We begin to see a shift towards acceptance of the queer community, which would only increase as we moved forward into the late 2000's and beyond. Queer cinema has grown exponentially since the 90's, and a few cult classics like But I'm a Cheerleader and A Beautiful Thing sowed the seeds to allow this to happen.

Conclusion

In preparation for writing this book, I watched upwards of 200 teen movies from the late 90's and early 2000s. Some of these were movies that I had seen before, many were old favourites. Others were films that I'd never watched prior to this time. Viewing all these teen movies pulled me back to my early teen years, to the time when watching a movie with my friends was the highlight of a Saturday night sleepover, when many lazy holiday afternoons were spent languishing in front of the VCR and checking out the latest offering from Video Ezy. It struck me how much the films I watched during this time informed my attitudes and beliefs about sex.

Now, I do need to point out that these films weren't the sole source of my sex education. I had a few formal sex education sessions at school, which mostly focused on anatomy and basic birth control. My parents provided me with plenty of books about sexuality and puberty, and while they made the offer that they were on hand to answer any questions I might have, I never really felt comfortable raising those queries with them. Like the characters in these films, I gleaned a lot of my sexual knowledge from my friends. When we were entirely inexperienced, we pooled what little knowledge we had, and then as we moved into our mid-to-late teen years the more experienced among us shared what they'd learned with those who had yet to dip a toe into the world of sexual experimentation. I also pieced together a patchwork of sexual knowledge from the sex scenes from romance novels and the sealed sections of Dolly magazine. At the time I felt like I had a fairly robust knowledge of sexuality, but in hindsight I realize that a lot of what I "knew" was dead wrong, and that there was a fair amount of vital information that was simply missing.

For me personally, what I absorbed from the movies from this time was a combination of tidbits about the mechanics of sex, as well as a lot of the beliefs I held about what sex was, when you should have sex, and when you shouldn't. I held very tightly to the idea that being a virgin was A Very Good Thing and that I should hold onto my virginity for as long as possible. It's funny because I have no recollection of anyone explicitly telling me this. This deep-seated belief wasn't based on any conversation with my parents or another trusted adult telling me that I should stay a virgin. I feel like the importance I placed on virginity was the product of countless tiny messages from a variety of sources, including the movies that I loved so much. I have looked back over journal entries that I made when I was 13 years old where I say that I intend to wait until I was married to lose my virginity. Later on, I relaxed this idea and decided that I might not wait until marriage, but that I certainly wanted my first time to have meaning, and that I would wait until the time was "just right" to have sex. Naturally, as a highly anxious teenager, I spent a lot of my time second guessing when the time would be "just right" and missed many, many opportunities to have great and meaningful sex because of my own internalized anxiety about the importance of virginity.

Around this time, I remember spending a lot of time reflecting on different movies and the scenes of virginity loss, of the triumphs and pitfalls of the various characters that I'd seen so many times. My mind became a tangle of pros and cons, of dos and don'ts, and it took me ages to make up my mind to finally have sex for the first time.

While I can't rewind the clock and do things differently, I do wonder from time to time if my attitudes to sex would have been different if I'd been given a more comprehensive sex education. I have to consider the possibility that if I'd been raised in a culture that was more sex positive, with more accessible information about sex, that the decision to begin having sex for the first time might not have been so fraught with anxiety for me. If I'd been able to consider my sexual debut as simply the first time I was going to experience something, rather than a monumental and life-altering event, I may not have agonized so much over the decision (and ultimately enjoyed the experience a little more when the time finally came). I have to concede that the media I was consuming during my teen years definitely played a huge part in making me feel like I needed to hold onto my virginity, and certainly contributed to my confusion and anguish when deciding whether or not to let it go. I do feel like if I'd had more cultural messages that countered these ideas and didn't place as much emphasis on the importance of virginity, I would have had a much easier time.

We've seen the ways that some of the movies from this time accurately reflect the sexual experiences of the teenagers who were exploring their sexuality at this time. And I've also pointed out some of the ways that the films get it wrong. Often, the missteps and misinformation occur as a result of the filmmaker making a joke, or exaggerating something for comedic or dramatic effect. And this in itself isn't problematic. Films are meant to be a source of entertainment, and rarely does a film manage to fully capture the experience of real life. If films were exactly like real life, they would be incredibly boring. Films need to be bigger, brighter and more sensational than our regular lives to hold our interest, to allow us to escape into a fantasy world. I have no problem with filmmakers choosing a more sensational representation of sexuality. What I do take issue with is a generation of teens who were so starved for sex education that they couldn't tell the difference between fantasy and reality, and that they sometimes relied on these films to fill the gaps in their own sexual knowledge. When teenagers don't have adequate sex education, they are more vulnerable to internalizing the messages about sex that they glean from popular media.

I've talked a lot throughout this book about the importance of comprehensive sex education. We know that when comprehensive sex education in taught in schools, from kindergarten all the way through to high school, that rates of teen pregnancy and STIs in teenagers are lower. Conversely, we know that abstinence-only education produces the opposite result. What we see is the importance of arming people with knowledge about their bodies and their sexuality. Giving children and teens accurate, age-appropriate information about sexuality empowers them to be able to make careful and informed choices about their own sexual experimentation. It gives them the ability to explore sex without taking huge risks and putting themselves in danger. When they have a support network of trusted adults that they can consult for information, they don't have to turn to media that is intended to entertain, rather than educate, to answer their questions.

If anything, what my research and experience writing this book has taught me is that we shouldn't be relying on films that are intended to entertain to be a source of education. When teenagers don't receive sufficient or accurate education about sex, when they aren't raised in an environment where there are trusted adults available to answer their questions, they turn to other sources for information. And this is why it's so important to provide comprehensive education about sex. Since the early 2000's, I feel that sexual education in schools has improved. Fewer schools are relying on abstinence-only education models. Now, with the increased accessibility of the internet, there are countless websites, podcasts and Youtube channels dedicated to providing accurate, sex positive education for people of all ages. If a teenager has a question about sex, there are plenty of reputable sources at their fingertips. There is less need than ever for teenagers to rely on the advice of their friends, or a magazine, or a movie to teach them what they need to know about sexuality. And as we move forward into a world with more accessible sex education content, we have a batch of teens who not only aren't relying on films to teach them about sex, but can be more discerning about the messages they see in contemporary teen movies.

It brings me so much joy to consider that contemporary teenagers have access to so much reliable information about sexuality. I feel like they will be able to avoid much heartache and confusion by virtue of this fact. I know from my own experience how challenging it is to grow up with a head full of questions about sexuality, but not being able to access the answers. How frustrating it can be to have a sex ed class that will teach you to put a condom on a banana, but which completely omits any discussion of LGBTQI+ sexual expression, pleasure, masturbation or consent. Friends have shared with me their experiences of making poor decisions around sex because they simply didn't have enough information to help them with their choices. Some of these decisions were merely ill-advised, whereas others were genuinely dangerous and put them at real risk. I know many people, myself included, who marched into adulthood thinking we knew a lot about sex, only to realize that we knew a lot less than we believed.

For me personally, a big part of exploring my sexuality as an adult has involved identifying the holes in my sexual knowledge, and unlearning so many of the lessons I learned as a teenager which were incorrect. Comprehensive sex education and the rise of accessible information aimed at teenagers has unburdened contemporary teenagers of the need to piece together crumbs of information to form an incomplete whole. It's given them the gift of reliable sexual knowledge, and a confidence that will allow them to make more informed choices about sex. It is my hope that, moving forward, we will continue to improve the dissemination of information about sex and sexuality to teenagers, and that we can continue to make teen movies that are a fantastic source of entertainment, without worrying about them giving "the wrong message" about sex.

References

Articles

Afifi, T. D., Joseph, A., & Aldeis, D. (2008). Why can't we just talk about it?: An observational study of parents' and adolescents' conversations about sex. *Journal of Adolescent Research, 23,* 689 – 721.

Calabia, A. (2001). Teens and Sex. *Psychology Today.* July 2001(7)

Corliss, A. R. (2017). I'd rather be a slut: An analysis of stigmatized virginity in contemporary sexual culture. *Bard Undergraduate Senior Projects.* 2017. https://digitalcommons.bard.edu/senproj_s2017/397

DeLemater, J. (1987). Gender Differences in sexual scenarios. In K. Kelley (Ed.), *Females, Males and Sexuality* (pp 127-40). Albany: State University of New York Press.

Fortenberry, J. D., Schick, V., Herbenick, D., Sanders, S.A., Dodge, B., & Reece, M. (2010). Sexual behaviours and condom use at last vaginal intercourse: a national sample of adolescents ages 14 to 17 years. *J Sex Med, 2010(7),* 305-314.

Gevers, A., Mathews, C., Cupp, P., Russell, M. & Jewkes, R. (2013). Illegal yet Developmentally Normative: A Descriptive Analysis of Young, Urban Adolescents' Dating and Sexual Behaviour in Cape Town, South Africa. *BMC International Health and Human Rights*, 31. pp1-10.

Greydanus, D. E., Huff, M. B., & Omar, H. A. (2012). Adolescent Pregnancy. In Greydanus, D. E., Patel, D. R.,

Omar, Fuecht, C., & Merrick, J. (Eds) *Adolescent Medicine: Pharmacotherapies in General, Mental and Sexual Health* (p 387-397). Walter de Greyter GmbH & Co.

Greydanus, D. E., & Omar, H. A. (2014). Adolescence and Human Sexuality. In Merrick, J., Tenenbaum, A. & Omar, H. A. (Eds.), *Adolescence and Sexuality* (pp 9-61). Nova Science Publishers Inc.

Greydanus, D. E., Seyler, J., Omar, H. A. & Dodich, C. B. (2012). Sexually Transmitted Diseases in Adolescence. *Paediatrics Faculty Publications.* p 134. University of Kentucky.

Higgens, J. A., Trussell, J., Moore, N. B., & Davidson, J. K. (2010) Virginity Lost, Satisfaction Gained? Physiological and psychological sexual satisfaction at heterosexual debut. *J Sex Res 2010(7)* 384-394

Jones, J., Salazar, L. F., & Crosby, R. (2015). Contextual Factors and Sexual Risk Behaviors Among Young, Black Men. *American Journal of Men's Health* 11(3). Pp 508-517.

Kim, L. L. (1999). Study: Teens Lack Facts on Sexual Health. *Atlanta Journal-Constitution.* October 20, 1999.

Kinsman, S. B., Romer, D., Furstenberg, F. F., & Schwarz, D. F. (1998). Early sexual initiation: the role of peer norms. *Pediatrics, 102(5)*, 1185-92.

Kunkel, D, Cope, K. M., & Biely, E. (1999). Sexual Messages on Television: Comparing Findings from Three Studies. *The Journal of Sex Research*, 36(3), 230-236.

Kuo, S.S. (2000). A Little Privacy, Please: Should We Punish Parents for Teenage Sex? *Kentucky Law Journal,* 88(1), 136-198.

LeBrun, S. & Omar, H. A. (2015). The Importance of Comprehensive Sexuality Education in Adolescents. *Dynamics of Human Health* 2(4).

Lipman, C. M. & Moore, A. J. (2016). Virginity and Guilt Differences Between Women and Men. *Butler Journal of Undergraduate Research* 2(25), 117-133

McElderry, D. H. & Omar, H. A. (2003). Sex Education in the Schools: What Role Does it Play? *International Journal of Adolescent Medicine and Health*, v15(1) pp 3-9.

Merrick, J., Tenenbaum, A. & Omar, H. A. (2014). Adolescence and Sexuality. In *Adolescence and Sexuality: International Perspectives*. Merrick, J., Tenenbaum, A., & Omar, H. A. (Eds). (pp 3-6). Nova Publishers Inc.

Men's Health Staff (2019) Pornhub Reveals the 10 Most Popular Porn Categories of the Last 10 Years. *Australian Men's Health*, 11 September 2019.

Omar, H. A., McElderry, D. H. & Zakharia, R. M. (2003). Educating Adolescents about Puberty: What are we Missing? *Paediatrics Faculty Publications.* p 83. University of Kentucky.

Pasley, K., & Gecas, V. (1984). Stressed and satisfactions of the parental role. *Personal and Guidance Journal, 62*, 400.

Planned Parenthood Federation of America. (2020). *How Effective is Pulling Out?* Retrieved from https://www.plannedparenthood.org/learn/birth-control/withdrawal-pull-out-method

Poole, E. (2014). Hey Girls, Did You Know? Slut Shaming on the Internet Needs to Stop. *University of San Fransisco Law Review*, 48, 221-260.

Sant'Anna, M. J. C., Catunda, J. K., Carvalho, K. A. M., Coates, V., & Omar, H. A. (2006). Pregnant Teenager Involvement in Sexual Activity and the Social Context. *The Scientific World Journal*, v. 6, 998-1007.

Sant'Anna, M. J. C., Carvalho, K. A. M., Melhado, A., Coates, V., & Omar, H. A. (2007). Teenage Pregnancy: Impact of the Integral Attention Given to the Pregnant Teenager and Adolescent Mother as a Protective Factor for Repeat Pregnancy. *The Scientific World Journal*, v. 7, 187-194.

Wingert, P. (1999). How to Talk to Kids About Sex. *Newsweek*. June 14, 1999. 80-81.

Theses

Carpenter, L. M. (1999). *Virgin Territories: The Social Construction of Virginity Loss in the Contemporary United States*. [Doctorate Thesis. University of Pennsylvania].

Christian, S. E. (2017). *Body Image and Sex: How Women's Body Image Influences and Impacts Sexual Experiences*. [Masters Thesis. University of Kentucky]. https://uknowledge.uky.edu/hes_etds/52

Cui, G. (2016). *Do Beliefs About Sex Behaviors Mediate The Link Between Parent-Adolescent Communication About Sex and Risky Sexual Behaviors?* [Masters Thesis. University of Kentucky]. https://uknowledge.uky.edu/hes_etds/47

Hendricks, M. T. (2014). *Knowing and Being Known: Sexual Delinquency, Stardom and Adolescent Girlhood in Midcentury American Film*. [Masters Thesis. University of Kentucky]. https://uknowledge.uky.edu/english_etds/14

Hockersmith, L. D. (2016) *Comprehensive Sexuality Education in Kentucky.* [Masters Thesis. University of Kentucky]. https://uknowledge.uky.edu/cld_etds/30

Jeffers. T. E. L. (2005). *"Should I Surrender?" Performing and Interrogating Female Virginity In Hollywood Films 1957-64.* [Doctorate Thesis. University of Warwick].

McGladrey, M. L. (2011). *Becoming Bodies: How Preadolescent Girls Consume and Produce Media in 21st Century America.* [Masters Thesis. University of Kentucky]. https://uknowledge.uky.edu/gradschool_theses/102

Mohamad, R. (2014). *The Effect of Television Watching on Condom use among 9th-12th Graders.* [Doctorate Thesis. University of Kentucky]. https://uknowledge.uky.edu/cph_etds/20

Norwick, J. G (2016). *"Don't Have Sex, You'll Get Pregnant and Die!": Female University Student's Experiences With Abstinence-Only Education.* [Masters Thesis. University of Kentucky]. https://uknowledge.uky.edu/hes_etds/35

Otto, K. (2020). *Does Parental Stress Influence Parent-Child Sexual Communication?* [Masters Thesis. University of Kentucky]. https://uknowledge.uky.edu/hes_etds/81

Poynter, H. (2014). *The Effectiveness of Sexual Education Programs on Teen Births Among Females With and Without a Family History of Teen Births.* [Doctorate Thesis. University of Kentucky]. https://uknowledge.uky.edu/cph_etds/11

Films

Abraham, M., & Bliss, T. (Producers) & Reed, P. (Director). (2000). *Bring it on* [Motion picture]. United States: Beacon Pictures.

Abrams, P., Gladstein, R. N., & Levy, R. L. (Producers) & Iscove, R. (Director). (1999). *She's All That* [Motion Picture]. United States: Tapestry Films.

Abrams, P., Levy, R. L., Panay, A., & Martin, J. K. (Producers) & Becker, W. (Director). (2002). *Van Wilder* [Motion picture]. United States: Myriad Pictures.

Avellan, E. (Producer) & Rodriguez, R. (Director). (1998). *The Faculty* [Motion picture]. United States: Miramax Films.

Bender, C., Spink, J. C., Ohohen, M., Vince, W., & Johnson, B. (Producers) & Kumble, R. (2005). *Just Friends* [Motion picture]. United States: New Line Cinema.

Berg, A., Mandel, D., Goldberg, D., & Marcus, J. (Producers) & Shaffer, J. (Director). (2004). *Eurotrip* [Motion Picture]. United States: Dreamworks Pictures.

Bevan, T., Fellner, E., & London, M. (Producers) & Lehmann, M. (Director). (2002). *40 Days and 40 Nights* [Motion Picture]. United States: StudioCanal.

Brooks, J.L., Mark, L., Colleton, S., Sakai, R., & Ansell, J. (Producers) & Marshall, P. (Director). (2001). *Riding In Cars With Boys* [Motion picture]. United States; Columbia Pictures.

Carli, A. (Producer) & Davis, T. (Director). (2002). *Crossroads* [Motion Picture]. United States: MTV Films.

Cartsonis, C., McFadzean, D., Whitcher, D., & Williams, M. (Producers) & Williams, M. (Director). (2000). *Where The Heart Is* [Motion Picture]. United States: 20th Century Fox.

Castleberg, J. (Producer) & Baumbach, N. (Director). (1995). *Kicking and Screaming* [Motion picture]. United States; Trimark Pictures.

Chadha, G. (Producer & Director). (2002). *Bend It Like Beckham* [Motion picture]. United Kingdom: Redbus Film Distribution.

Cohen, J., Gottesgen, L., & Schisgal, M. (Producers) & Iscove, R. (Director). (2000). *Boys and Girls* [Motion picture]. United States: Dimension Films.

Coppola, F. F. (Producer), & Coppola, S. (Director). (1999). *The Virgin Suicides* [Motion Picture]. United States: Paramount Classics.

Cort, R. W., & Madden, D. (Producers) & Carter, T. (Director) (2001). *Save The Last Dance* [Motion Picture]. United States: Paramount Pictures.

Creel, L., & Sperling, A. (Producers) & Babbit, J. (Director). (1999). *But I'm a Cheerleader* [Motion picture]. United States: Lions Gate Films.

Daniel, S., Jacks, J., & Mosier, S. (Producers) & Smith, K. (Director). (1995). *Mallrats* [Motion Picture]. United States: View Askew Productions.

Di Novi, D. (Producer), & Shankman, A. (Director). (2002). *A Walk To Remember* [Motion picture]. United States: Di Novi Pictures.

Feldsher, P., Burns, M., & Butan, M. (Producers) & O'Haver, T. (Director). (2001) *Get Over It* [Motion Picture]. United States: Ignite Entertainment.

Garnett, T., & Shapter, B. (Producers) & MacDonald, H. (Director). (1996). *A Beautiful Thing* [Motion picture]. United Kingdom: Sony Pictures Classics.

Goldberg, D., & Medjuck, J. (Producers) & Phillips, T. (Director). (2000). *Road Trip* [Motion Picture]. United States: Dreamworks Pictures.

Goldsmith-Thomas, E., Schindler, D., & Schiff, P. (Producers) & Newell, M. (Director). (2003). *Mona Lisa Smile* [Motion picture]. United States: Columbia Pictures.

Grazer, B (Producer) & Foley, J. (Director). (1996). *Fear* [Motion picture]. United States: Imagine Entertainment.

Halfon, L., Malkovich, J., Novick, M., & Smith, R. (Producers) & Reitman, J. (Director). (2007). *Juno* [Motion Picture]. United States: Mandate Pictures.

Hall, K. L., & Hoban, S. (Producers) & Fawcett, J. (Director). (2000). *Ginger Snaps* [Motion picture]. Canada: Motion International.

Heller, L., & Manulis, J, B. (Producers) & Kalvert, S. (Director). (1995). *The Basketball Diaries* [Motion picture]. United States: Island Pictures.

Isaac, S. & Junoven, N. (Producers) & Gosnell, R. (Director). (1999). *Never Been Kissed* [Motion picture]. United States: Fox 2000 Pictures.

Kershaw, R. (Producer) & Woods, K. (Director). (2000). *Looking for Alibrandi* [Motion picture]. Australia: Robyn Kershaw Productions.

Kirkpatrick, D., & Besman, M. (Producers) & Roos, D. (Director). (1998). *The Opposite of Sex* [Motion Picture]. United States: Rysher Entertainment.

Kliot, J., & Vincente, J. (Producers) & Isaacson, K. (Director). (2000). *Down to You* [Motion Picture]. United States: Miramax Films.

Konrad, C., & Woods, C. (Producers) & Craven, W. (Director). (1996). *Scream* [Motion Picture]. United States: Woods Entertainment.

Konrad, C., Plec, J., Weinstein, B., & Weinstein, H. (Producers) & Williamson, K. (Director). (1999). *Teaching Mrs Tingle* [Motion picture]. United States: Dimension Films.

Lazar, A. (Producer), & Junger, G. (Director). (1999). *10 Things I Hate About You* [Motion picture]. United States: Touchstone Pictures.

Lenkov, P. M., & Rotenberg, M. (Producers) & Rash, S. (Director). (1993). *Son in Law* [Motion picture]. United States: Buena Vista Pictures.

Levin, L., Lyons, J., Anderson, P. T., & Sellar, J. (Producers) & Anderson, P. T. (Director). (1997). *Boogie Nights* [Motion picture]. United States: New Line Cinema.

Levy-Hinte, J., & London, M. (Producers) & Harwicke, C. (Director). (2003). *Thirteen* [Motion Picture]. United States: Working Title Films.

Luhrmann, B., & Martinelli, G (Producers) & Luhrmann, B. (Director). (1996). *Romeo + Juliet* [Motion picture]. United States: Bazmark Productions.

Michaels, L. (Producer) & Waters, M. (Director). (2004). *Mean Girls* [Motion picture]. United States: Lorne Michaels Productions.

Milchan, A., Nathanson, M., Riche, A., & Ludwig, T. (Producers) & Moyle, A. (Director). (1995). *Empire Records* [Motion picture]. United States: Regency Enterprises.

Moore, C., & Zide, W. (Producers) & Rogers, J. B. (Director). (2001). *American Pie 2* [Motion picture]. United States: Universal Pictures.

Moore, D., & Todd, S. (Producers) & Glatter, L. L. (Director). (1995). *Now and Then* [Motion picture]. United States: New Line Cinema.

Moritz, N. H. (Producer) & Gallen, J. (Director). (2001). *Not Another Teen Movie* [Motion Picture]. United States: Sony Pictures Releasing.

Moritz, N. H. (Producer) & Kumble, R. (Director). (1999). *Cruel Intentions* [Motion picture]. United States: Original Film.

Mosier, S. (Producer) & Smith, K. (Director). (1997). *Chasing Amy* [Motion picture]. United States: Miramax Pictures.

Ohoven, M., Stern, S., Stipe, M., & Vince, W., (Producers) & Dannelly, B. (Director). (2004). *Saved* [Motion Picture]. United States: United Artists.

Pfeffer, R., Ufland, H. J., & Ufland, M. J. (Producers) & Stockwell, J. (Director). (2001). *Crazy/Beautiful* [Motion picture]. United States: Touchstone Pictures.

Polone, G., & Hofflund, J. (Producers) & Jann, M. P. (Director). (1999). *Drop Dead Gorgeous* [Motion Picture]. United States: New Line Cinema.

Robbins, B., Tollin, M., & Laiter, T. (Producers) & Robbins, B. (Director). (1999). *Varsity Blues* [Motion picture]. United States: MTV Productions.

Ross, G., Kilik, J., Degus, R. J., & Soderbergh, S. (Producers) & Ross, G. (Director). (1998). *Pleasantville* [Motion picture]. United States: New Line Cinema.

Rudin, S., & Lawrence, R. (Producers) & Heckerling, A. (Director). (1995). *Clueless* [Motion picture]. United States: Paramount Pictures.

Sharp, J., Hart. J., Kolodner, E., & Bienen, A. (Producers) & Peirce, K. (Director). (1999). *Boys Don't Cry* [Motion picture]. United States: Fox Searchlight Pictures.

Silverman, G., & Strauss, J. J. (Producers) & Decter, E. (Director). (2002). *The New Guy* [Motion picture]. United States: Columbia Pictures.

Simpson, D., & Bruckheimer, J. (Producers) & Smith, J. N. (Director). (1995). *Dangerous Minds* [Motion Picture]. United States: Buena Vista Pictures.

Topping, J., & Thomas, B. (Producers) & Kaplan, D., & Elfont, H. (Directors). (1998). *Can't Hardly Wait* [Motion Picture. United States: Columbia Pictures.

Tornell, L., & Kramer, S. (Producers) & Stein, D. (Director). (1999). *Jawbreaker* [Motion picture]. United States: Sony Pictures.

Traeger, M., & White, M. (Producers) & Cohn, A. (Director). (1998). *Dead Man on Campus* [Motion picture]. United States: Paramount Pictures.

Weitz, C., Weitz, P., Moore, C., Zide, W., & Perry, C. (Producers) & Wietz, P., & Weitz, C. (Directors). (1999) *American Pie* [Motion picture]. United States: Summit Entertainment.

About the Author

Vanessa Bowen is a writer and counsellor. Originally from Benalla in Victoria's North-East, she now calls Ballarat home.

Vanessa began publishing her writing on her blog in 2009. Originally focused on fashion and pop-culture, she soon turned to the topics of sexuality and mental health. Vanessa's work has been featured in a range of publications, including Kinke Magazine, Wellbeing Magazine and OzKink Fest. Apple Pies and Other Lies is Vanessa's first book, born from her love of 90's pop culture and passion for comprehensive sex-education.

In her spare time, Vanessa enjoys watching films, yarn crafts, thrifting and hanging out with her two cats: Freddie and Ringo.

Acknowledgements

Writing a book isn't something you can do all on your own. Many, many people contributed to the creation of this book.

My deepest thanks to my parents, for never flinching at forking out $5 and the Video Ezy card to foster my growing movie obsession from a young age.

A huge dollop of gratitude to Katherine Kitchener, for her valuable wisdom on writing and publishing.

Warmest regards to all of my friends, who acted as a sounding board and source of endless support during the writing of this book.

And finally, thanks to the wonderful crew at McDonalds for spending hours making those egg McMuffins, without which, I might never have finished this book.

www.ingramcontent.com/pod-product-compliance
Lightning Source LLC
Chambersburg PA
CBHW072131020426
42334CB00018B/1751